Advance Praise for
CAPE COD CONFIDENTIAL

"Here's a great, fresh way to connect to Cape Cod—through fascinating, personal, sometimes grisly stories that are far removed from typical tourist tales. There's nothing like strong writing about murder and mayhem to make a place come alive, and Evan Albright does just that."

> —Seth Rolbein, Editor, *The Cape Cod Voice*

"A jaunty tour through aspects of Cape Cod history—murders, mayhem, scams, and scamps—that are missing from the usual historical accounts. The perps here start with the Pilgrims and then range as high as a sitting US president and as low as anybody would want to go. Evan Albright has written a jaw-dropping narrative, laced with puns and sly humor, of a dreadful series of events. Don't read this book alone, in an isolated beach cabin, on a dark and stormy night."

> —Stephen Fox, author of *Blood and Power: Organized Crime in Twentieth-Century America*

"Chicken rustlers, clam nappers, investment fraud, unsolved murders, and bootleg banditry are just a few of Evan Albright's tales of famous and not-so-famous violations of the law that have occurred on our salty peninsula. If you've ever thought that life on today's Cape Cod is going to hell in a handbasket, you should have been around here for the crime wave of 1878!"

> —Jim Coogan, *Cape Cod Times* columnist and author of *Sail Away Ladies: Stories of Cape Cod Women in the Age of Sail*

Continued next page…

True tales
of murder,
crime, and
scandal from
the Pilgrims to
the present.

Cape Cod Confidential

By Evan J. Albright

Foreword by Paul Kemprecos

Cover design, interior design and typesetting by
Joe Gallante, Coy's Brook Studio, Harwich, MA
coysbrookstudio@comcast.net

Editorial, design and production supervision by Adam Gamble

Copyedited by Susan Bouse, Bouse Editorial, Lone Tree, CO

Printed in Canada

For more information, including special sales, please contact:

On Cape Publications
Toll free: 1-877-662-5839
www.oncapepublications.com
E-mail: ccconfidential@oncapepublications.com

Cover illustration depicting the battle between
Wampanoags and French explorers at Chatham Harbor
in 1606 is from Les Voyages dv Sievr de Champlain
Xaintongeois (The Voyages of Samuel de Champlain)
by Samuel de Champlain, 1612.
Reproduced by permission of the Houghton Library,
Harvard University.

DEDICATION

To my parents, who shared their love for the written word.

TABLE OF CONTENTS

FOREWORD

By Paul Kemprecos

One of the biggest challenges any fiction writer faces is the competition with real life. Truth is stranger than fiction. This may be an old cliché, but it is an undeniable fact that when it comes to the dark side, human inventiveness has no bounds.

The difficulty of coming up with crimes of the imagination that would not be overshadowed by actual headlines became apparent when I started writing fiction. The same year I began a book with someone being bound and gagged and thrown into the ocean, a robbery victim was tied up and tossed into the Cape Cod Canal. In another book I had a tame killer whale suspected in the death of his trainer, even though no orca had ever done such a thing. As I was writing the novel, a "tame" orca killed his trainer in a Canadian marine park.

It was with these experiences in mind that I urged my mystery class at Cape Cod Community College not to be conservative in their writing and to let their imagination run as loose as wildfire. To press the point, I brought in news clips of the Menendez trial, where two brothers, who had killed their parents in cold blood, sought sympathy on the grounds that they were orphans. The lovely autumn day I was working on a book that centered on a plot against the United States, two hijacked planes slammed into the Twin Towers.

As readers of *Cape Cod Confidential* will discover, the sandy sliver of land known throughout the world for its dunes, lighthouses, and lobster dinners is not immune when it comes to the maxim about truth versus fiction.

What Stephen King tale of terror could be more bizarre than the story of Charles Freeman, the religious fanatic who killed his four-year-old daughter Edith and invited the neighbors to dinner in the futile hope that she would rise from the dead? Could P. D. James have conjured up a monster like Jane Toppan, the jolly nurse who happily poisoned more than thirty people, including friends and family? And what better real-life soul mate for the fictional Hannibal Lecter than the Cape Cod vampire Tony Costa, who planted more in his remote garden than marijuana?

Evan "Josh" Albright has done a remarkable job of digging out these stories and others, and has written them in a humorous, entertaining style that will make you smile despite the grisly themes of some of the crimes. He goes back to the first murderous clash between tourists and locals. If you think things are bad now, just read the fatal encounter between the Indians and the French explorer Samuel de Champlain.

In the next 400 years, there would be many more crimes committed by Cape Codders and washashores alike. Although some were mundane, others reflected the uniqueness of the Cape itself, like Ruth McGurk, whose body was found in a bog, or the infanticide of Baby Doe with the strange ritual of "bier-right," when the victim can supposedly identify its murder.

Not all the stories involve violence. There is the account of the Mayflower descendant who proved to be a one-woman crime wave in Yarmouth. Then there was the rash of chicken thefts—and even stranger, pigeon thefts. There was the stolen church organ, and the cranberry thieves. Prohibition, with its midnight whiskey drops and homemade hooch, brought an entirely new dimension to the local crime scene.

The combination of crime and olde Cape Cod continues to exert a strong attraction for the public. Maybe it is the lonely beaches, the cloaking fogs, or that, despite its growth, there are parts of the Cape where no one can hear you scream.

Throughout its long history, the Cape has attracted pirates, mooncussers, witches, bootleggers, madmen, and mad women. Or those, like young fashion writer Christa Worthington, who simply wanted to get away from it all.

When Worthington was found stabbed to death in her remote Truro cottage, the murder made headlines around the world. The death exposed for all to see the seamy underside of a charming Cape Cod town.

Chances are that this story will continue to fascinate long after the murderer has been caught.

But that chapter will have to wait for *Cape Cod Confidential, Revisited*.

Paul Kemprecos is the author of the Aristotle "Soc" Socarides series of detective novels, for which he won the Shamus Award from the Mystery Writers of America. Along with Clive Cussler, Kemprecos has written four New York Times best-selling adventures of the NUMA files. Their most recent collaboration is Lost City. *Kemprecos lives in Dennisport with his wife, Christi.*

INTRODUCTION

The First Crime

"There is no crime on Cape Cod."
—Stephen O'Neil,
Falmouth police sergeant, 1988

Those were among the first words I heard when I moved to Cape Cod. I was a neophyte reporter for the *Enterprise* newspaper in Falmouth, assigned to cover the police department. Sergeant O'Neil, who had the distasteful task of answering questions from the press, made his pronouncement with tongue firmly in cheek.

As I was to learn over the next ten years as a reporter and editor, Cape Cod not only has its share of crime, it has crime that can only be described as damned peculiar. Here is a small sample of the type of stories that crossed my desk at the newspaper:

- A former member of the board of selectmen (the New England equivalent of a town council) is convicted of attempted murder after he tried to smash in his wife's skull with a brick.

- A retired fire chief is sentenced for leading a minor girl into prostitution. As he cools his heels in the state penitentiary, he collects a full disability pension (tax-free) from the county, which he was awarded fifteen years before, after claiming that pressure he received from the town finance committee when he was fire chief gave him a nervous breakdown. He failed to mention that another contributing factor might have been that one of the local cops had arrested him for exposing himself to little girls.
- Three brothers, two of them twins, execute a suicide pact in a boarded-up inn over looking the ocean. As there was only one gun, two of the brothers had to watch the third take the first bullet to his head.
- A battered wife speaks out against domestic abuse, garnering headlines across Cape Cod. A few months later she is arrested for allegedly running a prostitution ring and for soliciting men as "Kazuma the Tiger Woman."

These incidents occurred over the space of a single year, but more incredibly, they also occurred in the same town. Multiply these stories by 15 towns on the Cape, further multiplied by 400 years of Anglo habitation, and you can begin to see the wealth of material that awaited me.

A couple of years after my meeting with Sergeant O'Neil, I began researching what I thought would become a series of articles about strange crimes from Cape Cod's past. With only a little digging, that series stretched into a dozen articles, then

100, then 200. No crime on Cape Cod? The truth is that there has *always* been crime on Cape Cod.

Fifteen years before the Mayflower sailed for the New World, Pierre du Gua, the French governor of Acadia (today Eastern Canada and part of Maine), arrived at Cape Cod. Gua, along with two dozen of his best men, had left behind their tiny colony on St. Croisse Island in search of a new home. The French explorers had coasted south along the shores of Maine and Massachusetts before happening upon a beautiful landscape of glistening white sands, which they named "Cap Blanc." They were a couple of years too late. An Englishman, Bartholomew Gosnold, already had named this new land "Cape Cod" in honor of the fish he found in its waters.

The Gua expedition anchored in Nauset Harbor. The shoreline looked much as it does today, but instead of million-dollar homes there were summer huts belonging to the native Wampanoags. The Europeans brought with them a midsummer nor'easter that drove temperatures so low the explorers were forced to don their winter coats. The inclement conditions did not prevent Gua and his men from exploring. They visited a Wampanoag village and admired the crops of corn, beans, and tobacco. Everywhere the Gua expedition went, the Wampanoags accompanied them. Several joined Gua and his crew when they returned to their small barque.

Gua and his men had been exploring Canada and New England for two years. During that time, they encountered thousands of Indians without so much as a cross word between the races. That came to an end on Cape Cod.

Trouble began when some of the men went ashore to fetch fresh water. They had been only out of sight only for a few minutes when they suddenly reappeared in a dead run back to shore, screaming to their comrades on the small ship to open fire. Close on the heels of the sailors were several Wampanoags armed with bows and arrows.

Though they could not speak French, the Wampanoags on board the barque understood there was trouble and leaped overboard to safety. A couple of the sailors managed to grab and bind one of the natives. The rest of the crew raced to retrieve their muskets.

On the shore, the Wampanoags drew arrows and shot one of the fleeing sailors in the back. "Seeing this, they ran at once to him, and dispatched him with their knives," wrote a witness to the fight. By this time, several of the crew aboard the barque had readied their muskets and commenced firing. The noise drove off the attackers, and they disappeared into the woods, leaving behind their victim.

Before the encounter was over, history nearly was changed forever. One of the men on the barque had his musket blow up in his face. "New France" nearly lost its father, for the musketeer was none other than Samuel de Champlain, the future founder of Quebec. Champlain was cartographer and scribe for Pierre du Gua, and he now had the honor of writing Cape Cod's first crime report.

As Champlain told it, the skirmish began when one of the Wampanoags swiped a copper kettle from a sailor who was attempting to get fresh water—the first theft on Cape Cod. Another sailor gave chase, but failed to catch the fleet-footed thief.

Champlain's version of the story conveniently fails to explain how the theft of a pot escalated into a mad chase down the shoreline. Perhaps he did not know because he could not ask the victim of the kettle theft, who had the bad luck of also being Cape Cod's first murder victim. There must have been more to the story, for Gua decided to release the Wampanoag captive on the barque, "being persuaded that he was not to blame." A few hours later, a delegation of Wampanoags showed up to apologize for the fracas. They claimed another tribe farther in the interior of Cape Cod had stolen the pot.

Explorers at Chatham Harbor in 1606 as drawn by Samuel de Champlain. Reproduced by permission of the Houghton Library, Harvard University.

Champlain summed up the local Wampanoag character by noting, "they are great thieves and, if they cannot lay hold of any thing with their hands, they try to do so with their feet. ... It is necessary to be on one's guard against this people, and live in a state of distrust of them, yet without letting them perceive it." There is no record of what the Wampanoag thought of the French.

A glutton for punishment, Champlain returned to Cape Cod the next year, this time anchoring off what is today Chatham. Early one morning, a force estimated in the hundreds attacked, killing one sailor instantly, mortally wounding a second, and injuring three more.

Champlain and the men fired muskets at the attackers and hit no one. The crew buried their dead on the shore under a large, makeshift cross and returned to the barque. When the natives reappeared a few hours later, the Frenchmen tried to drive them off by firing a small brass cannon. This failed to impress the Wampanoags, who tore down the cross and dug up the corpses. When they started to build a fire to burn the bodies, the French decided they had seen enough and hurled themselves at the shore. The natives once again melted into the woods, leaving the white men to rebury their dead. The explorers left Cape Cod, but before they did, they named the little harbor Port Fortune "on account of the misfortune which happened to us there."

Historians speculate that the French abandoned any plans to settle on Cape Cod because of trouble with the natives. It may also be true that they sensed there was something not quite right about the place. The following pages document the countless other murders and thefts, as well as the frauds, bootlegging, break-ins, and assaults—all of them wonderfully strange and curious—that litter the long history of Cape Cod.

Death Takes a Holiday

Cape Cod in recent years has become as well known for its murders as for its sun, sand, and surf. In 2002, someone stabbed to death Christa Worthington, a former fashion writer, at her cottage in Truro. Newspapers and television reported the murder across the country, and the image that burned into everyone's mind was that of Worthington's infant daughter, who was alone with the body for almost two days. Worthington's tragic end was turned into a best-selling book, though the crime was, at the time of publication, unsolved.

The connection between Cape Cod and vivid accounts of homicide is not new, as this chapter reveals. The following stories contain almost a dozen murders over the course of a century. Each one exploded on the front pages of newspapers far beyond the soothing shores of Cape Cod.

The Curse of Charles Freeman

The death of little Edith Freeman was more than sixteen-year-old Mary Davis could bear. The horrible truth pounded heavily against her breast with every beat of her heart.

"Minnie," as Davis was known to her family and friends, lived in South Pocasset, an isolated part of the Cape Cod town of Sandwich.

Her father, Alden Davis, had been a forward thinker, one of those who recognized how trains were going to transform Cape Cod in the nineteenth century from a landscape, in the words of Emerson, "made of salt, dust, gravel and fish bones," into a holiday paradise. When the rail line opened to Woods Hole in the early 1870s, Davis staked out a place along its route and built a small hotel. He brought along his wife, Mary, and four children, of which Minnie was the eldest.

Though Alden Davis was not a Cape Codder by birth, his neighbors overlooked his flawed pedigree, and most regarded

Hattie and Charles Freeman

him well. He became South Pocasset's first postmaster and ran a side business of carving headstones. He was very religious, and many of those who came to patronize his small hotel were similarly inclined.

In the late 1870s, the Davises and eight other families split from the Methodist church to join a new Christian sect called the Second Adventist Church, which was sweeping New England. In truth, the families were cast out from the local church for their unconventional beliefs.

From their ranks grew a leader, Charles Freeman. He had moved to Cape Cod in 1874, but unlike Alden Davis, he came with a local connection. His wife, Hattie, was a Cape Codder by birth. He became a tremendous student of the Bible, and his fellow Second Adventists considered him their minister.

One spring day in 1879, Freeman announced that God desired of him to act on His behalf. Freeman did not say what God had been asking him to do, but he did say that the calling was so strong that he could neither sleep nor eat. He said

3

he would have a major announcement at the next meeting of the Second Adventists.

Everyone left assuming that Freeman had decided to give up his life as a Cape Cod farmer to become an itinerant preacher for the Second Adventist religion. No one was surprised when he summoned them to his home on May 1, 1879.

Minnie and her mother came to hear the good news. The small congregation listened to Freeman preach for about an hour. The lay minister was somewhat disappointed, for he had also invited town officials, and none had bothered to come. Undeterred, he led everyone into the next room to unveil his good news—the body of his four-year-old daughter, Edith.

Freeman explained that God had been telling him to make a sacrifice, just as He had commanded Abraham in the Old Testament. Freeman said he had been unclear exactly what that sacrifice must be, but the night before during a fierce

electrical storm it came to him—he had to kill his favorite, little Edith.

Later that night he revealed God's plan to his wife, and the couple prayed. Finally she said, "Charlie, do the Lord's will." Freeman dressed and, singing religious songs, went out to his shop to retrieve a knife. "I never felt so happy in my life," he said later. Freemanwalked up the stairs to the

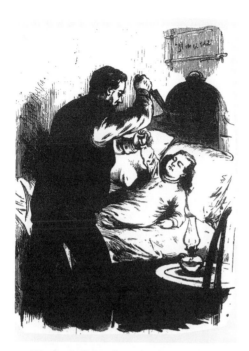

bedroom shared by his two daughters. He carried a lamp in one hand and the large knife in the other. He placed the light on a chair next to Edith's bed. Freeman turned down her covers and raised the knife. In recalling the moment a few days later, he said that he expected God to send an angel to stop him, as He had done for Abraham. No angel came, and Freeman plunged the knife into his daughter's side. She woke, looked up at him and cried, "Oh, father." Freeman gathered her into his arms and held her until she died.

Freeman told the Second Adventists to expect a miracle, that God would raise his daughter in three days. The meeting broke. No one spoke out against Freeman's "sacrifice." They all agreed it was "a strange event that they could not understand."

Everyone went home to await the miracle. That evening Minnie received a visit from a suitor, Constable Seth Redding. In tears, she told him of the sacrifice, and the next day Redding arrested Freeman and his wife. The murder was a sensation, and accounts of it appeared in newspapers across the country and in Europe.

Alden Davis stood up for his friend Charles Freeman. "What I propose to say will be in defense of, and from love to, the father and mother now in jail for the horrid crime," Davis told a crowd of 200 a couple of days later. "The world wants to know the motives of this man. None know them better than I do. I can vouch for it that there never lived a purer man than Charles Freeman."

While one could, in some twisted way, commend Davis's loyalty to his friend, few could admire his sense of timing. Davis had chosen to loudly proclaim his loyalty at the funeral of little Edith, as mourners were gathered around her freshly dug grave, her tiny cas-

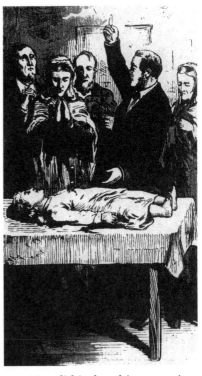

ket resting open atop the vault. Several mourners were almost provoked to violence, but Davis and family managed to escape to harangue another day.

A judge sent Charles Freeman to the insane asylum. Alden Davis voluntarily followed him, although his stay was relatively brief. Davis was soon good as new and back to running his little hotel next to the tracks. Throwing one's support behind a filicidal maniac apparently was not bad for business. Nor did it dent his reputation among his peers, for he was elected several times as Cataumet's representative to the school committee.

Four years later, Freeman was returned to Cape Cod. On May 1, the anniversary of the murder of little Edith, several experts testified before the Supreme Judicial Court that Freeman was now sane. The court ordered him held until the next seating of the grand jury, which would determine whether he would stand trial.

Two weeks later, on May 16, the Davis family was rocked by the death of the only son, Henry. Three weeks after that, daughter Bessie also died. It was as if the return of Charles Freeman had cursed the Davis family. If it was a curse, it would haunt them for the rest of their lives. But that is another story.

And what of Charles Freeman? On December 5, 1883, months after Henry and Bessie Davis were buried not far from little Edith, Freeman stood trial for the murder of his daughter. The jury found him not guilty by reason of insanity. Even though experts had proclaimed his sanity restored, the judge ordered him returned to asylum, where he was to spend the rest of his life.

Jolly Jane

Even as far back as 1901, Halloween was a day celebrated by children—but not by a small boy from the Cape Cod village of Pocasset. Ten-year-old Jesse Gibbs would have found the mock horrors of the holiday too much to bear. He probably had no desire to dress as a monster. Unlike his friends, he knew that real bogeymen were not swathed in the costume of the grotesque, but garbed in the raiment of angels.

When his mother had lain dying only two months before, Jesse had gone to such an evil seeking comfort. He had lain in its bed and cried on its breast. Although he did not know it at the time, his fears had been soothed by a demon who, once Jesse had fallen to sleep, rose from the bed to slowly draw the life from his mother who lay senseless nearby.

Now, on All Hallows' Eve, the evil had been contained, captured in New Hampshire and locked in the Barnstable County Jail. Jane Toppan did not look like the worst monster

MISS JANE TOPPAN LEFT THE COURT HOUSE LEANING ON THE ARM OF HER ATTORNEY

ever to walk the sandy shores of Cape Cod. She was a plump, middle-aged woman who was so frightened she could barely walk the 200 feet from her cell to the courthouse where she was arraigned for the murder of Jesse's mother. As she shuffled toward the courtroom, she leaned heavily on state police Detective Simeon Letteney, looking as if she might collapse any moment. Once inside, she was asked if she had murdered Jesse's mother. "Not guilty," Jane Toppan replied, her voice trembling. She was returned to her cell. The entire proceeding took only three minutes.

The idea that this meek-looking woman, a professional nurse, could kill another human being was incredible. But according to the newspapers, and the talk around the Cape, Jane Toppan had not only murdered Jesse's mother, but also his aunt and his grandparents. She had poisoned all four over the course of the summer, they said. Cape Cod experienced a true sense of déjà vu, when newspapers printed the list of victims: Mary (Davis) Gibbs, better known as Minnie; Genevieve (Davis) Gordon, Minnie's younger sister; Mary Davis, Minnie's mother; and Alden Davis, her father. Twenty-two years earlier, these names were linked to another horrible act, the murder of little Edith Freeman by her father, Charles.

Charles Freeman had been a trusted friend of the Davis family, and so, too, was Jane Toppan. In Boston and Cambridge, no private nurse was more respected than Toppan. In those two cities, some of the most prominent physicians in the world resided and practiced. Many doctors considered her the best nurse with whom they had ever worked; patients adored her, not only for her skill in nursing, but also for her sunny disposition, which more than one person described as "jolly."

Beginning in 1896, for the five years leading up to her arraignment, Jane Toppan had spent her summers in South Pocasset, an area now known as Cataumet, renting a cottage from Alden and Mary Davis. By 1901, the Davises were in semiretirement and had converted their small inn, the Jachin Hotel, into the family home. They continued to rent several cottages on their property, and one of their favorite summer guests in recent years had been Jane Toppan. But favorite did not mean "free," and the Davises became concerned in 1901 when Jane came to owe them $450 in back rent.

In late June, before the summer visitor season officially began, Mary Davis decided to travel to Jane's home in Cambridge and collect the back rent. For someone sixty-three and in failing health, a trip by rail to Boston and Cambridge could be most taxing. The day promised to be unseasonably warm, which would place an added strain upon the old woman. What persuaded her to make the trip was that daughter Genevieve would be coming in by train that day from Chicago for her annual summer visit.

Mary Davis never returned to Cape Cod alive. She collapsed and fell into a coma in Cambridge. Five days later, she was dead. A doctor attributed her demise to diabetes.

On the return trip to Cape Cod, Mary Davis's body rode in the baggage compartment. Jane Toppan, who had been invited by the rest of the Davis family to attend the funeral, took her seat in the passenger car.

The Davis clan gathered in the days following Mary Davis's death. Genevieve was there, with her daughter, who was named after her mother. Sister Minnie, who had wed a Cape Cod ship captain, closed her house in the nearby village of Pocasset and moved in, along with her two boys, Paul and Jesse. Alden Davis, of course, was there. And finally, Jane Toppan, who proved to be just the tonic the Davis family needed. She kept everyone's spirits up with her delightful stories and caring words.

In spite of Jane's ministrations, the family was kept on edge throughout July. A series of mysterious fires broke out in the former hotel and adjoining buildings. In each case, the flames were extinguished before they could cause serious damage.

Genevieve became more and more anxious in the days following her mother's death. Foremost in her mind was the health and sanity of her father, who was emotionally shattered after losing his wife. Her husband, Harry, was in Chicago, and she was lonely and depressed.

A few weeks after Mary Davis's funeral, Jane Toppan went to Minnie Gibbs to report that she had overheard Genevieve threatening to kill herself. On the evening of July 28, Genevieve mysteriously took ill. By morning, she was dead. Jane hinted that Genevieve had poisoned herself with an insecticide made of arsenic and copper called "paris green," which was kept in a shed on the property. Dr. Leonard Latter, the local physician, wrote on the death certificate that heart disease had killed Genevieve. It is not known if he had been told anything about a possible suicide.

Cataumet had its second Davis funeral in less than a month. Preparations for it had driven Alden Davis into a state of frenzy. He was enraged that the coffin company would not sell him one of its models at wholesale. Sometime after the funeral, Davis took the train to Boston to visit the daily newspapers, looking to get them to print a letter he wrote about the nefarious "coffin trust."

Alden Davis was nearly seventy and in questionable mental and physical health. In spite of his infirmities, he appeared fit when he went to bed on the evening of August 8. Early the next morning, Jane reported to others in the house that she had found Davis dead in his bed. The family sent once again for Dr. Latter. The aged physician determined his patient had died of apoplexy.

Harry Gordon, Genevieve's husband, had come for his wife's funeral and now attended the same ceremony for his father-in-law. Two days after Alden Davis's death, Harry went to Minnie, now the sole surviving Davis, and urged her to have a talk to Jane Toppan about the money she owed the family. Minnie did speak to Jane, although it is not known what transpired in that conversation. The next day, Minnie went for a carriage ride in Falmouth and returned in good spirits. That night she was overtaken with illness and by nine o'clock the next morning was in a stupor from which she never recovered.

Over the course of seven weeks, Jolly Jane Toppan had poisoned to death the entire Alden Davis family. And no one living in Cataumet had the slightest suspicion, perhaps because of a lingering belief that the Davis family was cursed as a result of their involvement in the "Pocasset Filicide," as the Edith Freeman murder was known.

The state police, however, did not believe in curses. They had been tracking Jane Toppan for some time, believing that she was responsible for murdering several of her patients. In late August, men unearthed the remains of Minnie and her sister, Genevieve, in the Cataumet cemetery. The bodies were removed to a nearby barn, which had been transformed into a makeshift morgue. Dr. R. H. Faunce, the medical examiner for Barnstable County, dissected the two women and removed their internal organs, which were given to eminent Harvard pathologist Edward Wood. He found poison, and police ordered Jane arrested.

Boston, with more than a dozen newspapers, turned the Jane Toppan murders into a sensation. Reporters tripped all over themselves digging into Jolly Jane's background, which, they soon found, was littered with corpses. Within two weeks, the estimate of Jane's victims climbed into the double digits.

She confessed the day before her trial in the spring of 1902. To everyone's surprise, she admitted to more murders than even the newspapers had suspected. "There were 31 in all," she told her lawyer, but added that there were probably many more. "My memory is not very good; I forget some things." She also confessed to setting the fires at the Davis compound.

At her trial, which was solely for the murder of Mary Gibbs, Attorney General Herbert Parker handled the prosecution. He could not produce any murder weapon or

JANE TOPPAN HEARS THE JURY'S VERDICT.

SKETCHES AT TRIAL OF JANE TOPPAN FOR MURDER AT BARNSTABLE.

demonstrate any motive. Of course, he had her confession, which Jane had given to several psychologists.

Jane had told them that she received a sexual thrill from poisoning her victims. The psychologists decided that Jane was insane. A jury deliberated ninety minutes before coming back with their verdict—not guilty by reason of insanity. She was ordered to the state asylum for the insane in Taunton.

Why did Jane confess when the evidence against her was so weak? One reason may have been that she believed she would eventually be released from the insane asylum. How could she ever reach the conclusion that such a well-known murderer would ever be freed?

Simply. It had been done before. Alden Davis's good friend, Charles Freeman, who had murdered his own child in 1879, had been ordered to spend the rest of his life behind asylum walls. In 1888, friends of Charles Freeman petitioned for his freedom on the grounds he had been found sane, and the governor ordered Freeman released. Jane Toppan knew of the Charles Freeman case, not only through her connection with the Davis family, but also through her own "alienist" (as psychiatric professionals were known at the time), who had been one of the doctors who proclaimed Freeman cured.

Jane confession of moral insanity saved her from the electric chair, but she did not share the same fate as Charles Freeman. She died at the Taunton Asylum in 1938, a sweet old lady that many described as "jolly."

First to Fry

The prosecution of Edwin Ray Snow for murder was fixing to be the trial of the century. True, the century would be only a few hours old when Snow faced charges of first-degree murder on January 1, 1900. If convicted, seventeen-year-old Snow would become the first man in Massachusetts to die in the electric chair.

Snow stood accused of the cold-blooded murder of a shirttail relative, Jimmy Whittemore. On September 12, 1899, Snow accompanied Whittemore on the latter's delivery route for a Dennis bakery. The two young men made an odd pair. The nineteen-year-old Whittemore was mature beyond his years. When his father had died a couple years before, he automatically assumed responsibility for putting food on the table for his widowed mother and siblings. Eddie Snow, by comparison, was a ne'er-do-well. He had been left as a baby on a doorstep in Holyoke and adopted by the Snow family

Edwin Ray Snow

when he was five. He spent his teenage years in trouble. A conviction for breaking and entering earned him almost a year in the Concord reformatory, where he spent his time reading literature. Snow was allergic to hard work, and in early September had quit a job in Taunton and returned to the Cape.

The two young men were last seen together atop Whittemore's bread delivery truck at around 5:30 p.m., just before they turned onto a dirt path that cut through the woods between Yarmouth and South Yarmouth. The next morning, a group of men cutting through the Yarmouth woods on their way to work found Whittemore's body along the side of the dirt road. He had been shot twice and run over by a wagon.

The police force on Cape Cod was small and relatively unsophisticated, but it didn't take a lot of detective work to finger a suspect. Before the day was out, Cape Cod's sole state police detective arrested Edwin Ray Snow in Middleboro.

Eager reporters from all over New England descended upon the courthouse in Barnstable to watch Snow's march to the electric chair. The trial opened shortly after noon on Monday, New Year's Day 1900. Snow's defense lawyer had spent the morning attempting to negotiate a plea of murder in the second degree with the attorney general, who came down from Boston to prosecute the case. But negotiations had broken down, and the charge of first-degree murder, with its automatic sentence of death, remained.

Experienced court watchers expected the defense to seek a one-week continuance. To the surprise of almost everyone, Attorney General Knowlton announced to the judge that Snow had changed his plea. When ordered, the seventeen-year-old rose. His baby face betrayed no emotion, and he stood casually with his hands in his pockets as if he were lounging on a street corner. After the clerk read the indictment, the judge asked Snow if he wished to retract his plea of not guilty. "I do," he said in a loud, clear voice. "I desire to plead guilty to murder in the first degree."

Judge John Aiken then ordered that Snow be sent to the Charlestown State Prison and on March 18 be killed in the electric chair. The entire trial took less than a half hour. Edwin Ray Snow became the first man in the United States to be sentenced to death in the twentieth century and the first man in Massachusetts sentenced to be executed with electricity.

The chair had been ready for a year. Massachusetts was no pioneer in the use of electricity to enforce the death penalty. New York had been electrocuting murderers for almost a decade and had even executed its first woman only a few months earlier. Massachusetts's penal authorities admired New York's electric chair so much they built one exactly like it.

The state added a special wing to the prison in Charlestown, eighty feet long, thirty feet wide, and twenty feet high. The walls were twenty-eight inches thick, and the entire building was windowless except for several narrow slits in the ceiling that allowed limited sunlight and ventilation. It contained three large cells—a "murderer's row"—and the death chamber.

Snow arrived on January 15. Within a week, Governor Murray Crane commuted his sentence to life in prison. This had been part of the deal from the beginning. Snow only agreed to plead guilty to murder in the first degree if there was no chance he would face the automatic penalty of death by electrocution.

Although Snow was the first man sentenced to the electric chair, the honor of being its first victim fell to Luigi Storti, an Italian immigrant in Boston convicted of murdering a man who won the hand of a woman in the old country whom Storti had been courting. He died in the electric chair on December 17, 1901. Snow, on the other hand, served thirty-two years. During his confinement, Cape Cod had its share of murders, but none of the perpetrators ended up on death row. The governor pardoned Snow in 1932, the same week a Cape Cod court convicted Sylvester Fernandes, a Mashpee man, of murder and bestowed upon him the dubious honor of becoming the first and only Cape Codder to die in the electric chair (see "Dead Man Walking, Cape Cod Style," later in this volume). On April 21, Snow walked out of Charlestown State Prison a free man. He had all of America in front of him and eventually ended up in California. For Fernandes, the man who took his place on "murderer's row," the walk was somewhat shorter.

The Vacationist in the Bog

The hottest tourist spot on Cape Cod was not on the Cape at all. The village of Onset sits at the head of Buzzards Bay in Wareham, the self-described "Gateway to Cape Cod," and during the 1940s it was the premier visitor destination in Southeastern Massachusetts. There was a long, beautiful beach next to the state pier, a movie house, restaurants, and plenty of attractions where tourists could spend their time and spend their dimes.

All that changed in the summer of 1946. The demise of tourism in Onset began on July 19, a truly beautiful day. This was the first summer after World War II, and life was getting back to normal. During the lunch hour, plumbers working in the basement of Christie's Spa, a popular restaurant, broke the natural-gas line. The owner called the gas company, which promptly sent a serviceman to shut off the gas. Police evacuated the building and surrounded it with a safety rope. Shortly before one o'clock the gas-company employee fixed the leak. The fire department and gas company sounded the all clear, and the police removed the rope. A Cape Cod man, Raymond Brune, went back to work in the restaurant, where he was servicing the music box.

A few minutes later, the building containing the restaurant rose into the air as if lifted by a giant hand. An explosion blew it apart along with the three other buildings on the block. The blast killed Ray Brune and eight others, and sent a shower of glass, metal, and wood over the hundreds of visitors and residents in the area. "The building looked as if a 500-pound bomb had struck it," one witness said.

In retrospect, the explosion under Christie's Spa was a portent. That nine people had died was a tragedy, but it was an accident, an act of God. What would happen to Ruth McGurk was much, much worse—a malevolence wrought by the hand of man. The village of Onset was soon to be rocked by a different kind of explosion that would rend the very seams of the carefree vacation spot.

She arrived in Onset for a week's vacation a week after the explosion. Ruth McGurk was a shop clerk in Cambridge, Massachusetts. Being betrothed to a sailor who was stationed in the Bikini atoll in the Pacific did not prevent her from enjoying the nightlife for which Onset was so famous. The village had returned to normal except for the one destroyed block.

Ruth was vacationing with two girlfriends. One night, they headed over to the Colonial Casino dance hall. Ruth appeared to be dancing with one man in particular. At the end of the set, Ruth approached her friends' table. "I'm going out with Frank for a little while, but I'll be home early," she told them. "If I'm not home when you get there wait up for me." Ruth rejoined the man she called Frank, and the couple strolled down the steps of the pavilion and vanished.

A few days later, the local newspaper reported McGurk's disappearance with the headline, "Onset Vacationist Feared

Abducted." The next day the headline changed to "Woman's Body Found in Bog." Ruth McGurk's corpse had been found in a reservoir used to flood cranberry bogs, some eight miles from Onset. She was wearing the same pink dress she had worn to the Colonial Casino. On one hand was a diamond engagement ring, on the other an amethyst birthstone ring. Her shoes and undergarments were missing, police said. She had been beaten, strangled, and raped, her lifeless body tossed into the water. The search was on for "Frank."

Five days later, authorities arrested Charles Russell Goodale, twenty-five, a World War II navy veteran who resided in Onset. Police initially had charged Goodale with the attempted rape of another woman, but during the interrogation they came to the conclusion he was the "Frank" who murdered Ruth McGurk. A judge ordered Goodale held without bail.

Goodale's trial in Plymouth Superior Court began on May 12, 1947, nine months after his arrest. District Attorney Edmund R. Dewing presented a compelling case. Ruth's two girlfriends testified that Goodale was the man Ruth called Frank. At the time of the crime, Goodale lived with his parents. A lodger in that house testified he was at the Colonial Casino and saw Goodale with a woman who matched the description of Ruth McGurk. Another lodger told the court that he saw Goodale come home at 1:30 a.m. Another witness described how he and Goodale had at one time worked a cranberry bog less than a half mile away from the reservoir where Ruth's body was discovered. Another coworker of Goodale's testified that the defendant liked to disguise his identity and go by the name "Frank." He also provided the one detail that sticks to this day in the minds of New Englanders who remember the trial—Goodale had removed the handle on the passenger's door so that his romantic conquests could not escape. When police searched Goodale's car, it was missing the door handle. They also found three strands of hair similar in color to Ruth McGurk's.

Although the district attorney could not pin down a motive and the physical evidence connecting Goodale and McGurk was limited to a single hair, he had produced enough witnesses to link the two. Leading the defense team was Herbert Callahan of Boston, considered one of the best defense lawyers in New England. Callahan, tall with a shock of white hair atop his head, demolished the district attorney's case. For every witness the D.A. produced who saw Goodale with McGurk, Callahan presented witnesses who testified they saw Goodale either alone, with a group of friends, or with a woman who was not Ruth McGurk. At the start of the trial, Callahan told the press that he had been called by a woman who had been with Goodale that night. He never produced that witness, but his story made front-page news, so he could be certain the jury saw it. Another defense witness said she had sold Goodale his car and the door handle had been missing when she sold it. Several women testified they had taken rides in Goodale's car, so that the hair found could have been theirs. A police officer testified that McGurk's two companions had identified a completely different man as Frank when he interviewed them.

Callahan's coup de grâce was the defendant himself. Goodale took the stand and denied all the charges. He was a handsome young man, and a veteran, which could not have been lost on a jury that had lived through four years of world war. He told the jury that he had been at the Colonial Casino that night, along with hundreds of other men and women. He did dance with a woman (not Ruth McGurk), and he later drove her to the next town to have a beer. Afterward, he drove her back to Onset, and that was the last he ever saw of her.

Before the case went to the jury, the judge gave Goodale the opportunity to speak. "Gentlemen of the jury," he started, "Ever since this charge was first placed against me I have been hoping and praying that the girl I was out with would come forward. Why she has not, I do not know. I tell you men that I never met Ruth McGurk in my life, I swear to God I never killed her."

The jury deliberated for more than a day, but they were able to reach a decision. Not guilty.

The locals in Onset will tell you that tourism died with Ruth McGurk. Goodale's acquittal meant only one thing—there was still a murderer on the loose.

The Cape Cod Vampire

Everyone alive today who was on Cape Cod in 1969 remembers the gruesome murders of four young women discovered in the Truro woods.

Police discovered the first body, Susan Perry's, on February 8 when they were looking for the remains of two other women, Patricia Walsh and Mary Anne Wysocki. Perry had disappeared the previous Labor Day. They found her body in eight pieces and ravaged by decomposition. A month later, police found Wysocki's head and torso along with the body of Walsh in a large hole not far from a cleared plot that had once grown marijuana. Underneath these remains was the dismembered, decomposed cadaver of another woman, Sidney Monzon.

The medical examiner determined that someone had mutilated the bodies with a knife, but after shooting the victims to death.

The four women had known, in varying degrees, Antone Charles "Tony" Costa of Provincetown. Costa, authorities learned, was intimately familiar with the area where the bodies had been found. The remains of a marijuana patch belonged to Costa, and he had used the area as a hiding place for his drugs.

What had led authorities to the woods in the first place had been the discovery of an abandoned Volkswagen van that belonged to Walsh. Not far from the van, police found a torn cover of Volkswagen van owner's manual. Police laboratory tests identified Costa's fingerprints on it.

While the discovery of the bodies caused a sensation, the district attorney, Edmund Dinis, turned the case into a media firestorm. "The hearts of each girl had been removed from the bodies and were not in the graves, nor were they found," Dinis announced at a press conference. "A razor-like device was found near the graves. Each body was cut into as many parts as there are joints." Dinis also said that teeth marks had been found on the bodies.

When a reporter asked if this was the work of a "Cape Cod vampire," Dinis nodded. And with that, the media furor had suddenly been whipped into a frenzy.

While Dinis's comments made for great copy, they were untrue. The hearts had not been removed, although some organs were missing from at least one of the bodies. No cutting device had been found, and the remark about as many body parts as joints was wild hyperbole, if not physically impossible.

Dinis managed to transform the murders into an international story. Reporters from all over the nation came to Cape Cod. "The press is bad," Provincetown Police Chief Berrio said, "but the tourists are even worse." Antone Costa's "garden" had become a tourist trap (something that reportedly continues to this day). Curiosity seekers flocked to the Truro woods, hoping to find the graves or worse—one of the victim's joints that had been overlooked by police. Rumors of satanic worship began to shroud the case.

Cape Cod Confidential

Costa was tried and convicted of two of the murders in May 1970. His lawyer attempted to paint him as psychotic, but Costa would have none of that. At the conclusion of his trial, the alleged murderer gave a rational, intelligent speech to the jury that must have convinced them he was not only a killer but also terribly sane. The judge sentenced him to spend the rest of his life at the state prison in Walpole. The "rest of his life" amounted to only four years. Prison guards found his lifeless body, dead of an apparent suicide, in his cell on May 12, 1974.

Costa never confessed to the killings, unless you happen to subscribe to Daniel Webster's belief that "suicide is confession." The closest he came to admitting his involvement in the deaths of the four women was in *Resurrection*, a "factual novel" about the killings that he wrote while in prison. According to *Resurrection*, Costa did not commit the murders; responsibility for their deaths fell to "Carl," a pseudonym that Costa used for a friend. Carl allegedly shot Mary Anne Wysocki and Patricia Walsh in the Truro woods. Susan Perry and Sydney Monzon supposedly died of drug overdoses, one in the woods and the other in Carl's apartment. Both were dismembered after their deaths, Costa claimed, and buried later. In the case of the latter two women, Costa's novel claimed he had no involvement in their deaths other than the knowledge that they had happened.

Two months after Costa's body found its final resting place, a thirteen-year-old girl walking her dog in the dunes of the Cape Cod National Seashore in Provincetown came upon a nude woman's body, lying on half of a beach towel. Her killer had severed her hands (they were never found) and apparently tried to do the same with the head, but gave up and instead rested it upon the victim's folded jeans. As of this writing, police have been unable to identify the victim, so she goes by the romantic name "The Lady of the Dunes." Her killer is equally unknown and at large, although police can say with complete certainty that Tony Costa was never a suspect.

Demon Rum

The Cape sticks out into the Atlantic like an outstretched hand seeking spare change for a bottle of fortified wine. Cape Codders have always been a thirsty people.

The following tales have the pursuit of alcohol at their center, but in truth that is not what this chapter is about. As any alcoholic will tell you, the fight between sobriety and inebriation is never about the bottle, but the battle. The fight is never over booze but instead about prejudice between cultures, the search for the almighty dollar, the fiery relationships between men and women, and, as our first story illustrates, about cats.

The Cats Who Were Still Sniffing

The problem with Provincetown is not the wind, not the sand, not the scarcity of potable water. No, the problem with Provincetown is cats.

When the misanthropic naturalist Henry David Thoreau stopped there for the night in the early summer of 1857, cats were all he could talk about. The innkeeper at the Pilgrim House had given Hank a crowded little room in the attic, "though it was not crowded," he wrote sarcastically in his journal. There was only one window, "twenty and a half inches by twenty-five and a half ... and it required a chair to look out conveniently." This, truly, was the hotel guest from hell. There can be no satisfying the customer that brings his own yardstick to measure windows.

"Fortunately," the bard of Walden wrote, "it was not a cold night and the window could be kept open, though at the risk of being visited by cats, which appear to swarm on the roofs of Provincetown like the mosquitos on the summits of its hills."

Over eight years, Thoreau spent a total of four nights in Provincetown, an experience that added greatly to his knowledge of the natural history of feral cats.

"Every now and then one of these animals on its travels leaped from a neighboring roof on to mine." The noise was " as if a six-pounder had fallen within two feet of my head ... and then followed by a scrambling as banished sleep for a long season."

Cats apparently did not bother Provincetowners any, for it took a full eighty years before they got around to doing something about them.

In the fall of 1937, the Animal Rescue League announced it would begin a cat-trapping campaign in the Cape-tip community. Box traps would be set out throughout the town, the stray cats collected and taken away (perhaps to Walden?).

After several days of hunting, the cat trappers made their way to Franklin Street. They stopped at two homes, that of a sixty-three-year-old grandmother named Josephine Souza and of her neighbor down and across the street, John Burgess. The cat trappers, named William Carlos and Wendell Frost, asked permission from Mrs. Souza and Mr. Burgess to place cat traps in their respective back yards. Neither, it appeared, had read Thoreau, and therefore probably did not know that stray cats were part of the natural bestiary of Provincetown. They readily gave their permission.

A few days later, an army of local, state, and federal police descended on the Burgess and Souza households. Armed with warrants, the authorities searched both houses and surrounding grounds, and discovered that more had been cooking on Franklin Street than fish cakes and oyster pie.

At Mrs. Souza's home, police discovered nineteen pints of illegal moonshine. It turned out that Mrs. Souza was not only a retailer, but a manufacturer as well. In her house, police found a still cooking some thirty gallons of prune and oats mash (a concoction that was not only 100 proof, but high in fiber as well). Over at the Burgess household, police found a twenty-gallon still in the woodshed and twenty-five gallons of delicious "fruit-and-feed mash."

At one of the houses, police stumbled upon a "well-known former town employee" who had a pint of illegal hooch in his shirt pocket and thirty-five cents on the table in front of him.

The moonshiners had been sniffed out by the cat trappers, who, as it happens, were not cat trappers at all, although never did two cats operate more slyly than Carlos and Frost. William Carlos was a patrolman in the Provincetown Police Department; Wendell Frost was a trooper in the state police. For weeks before, federal agents had been trying to sniff out stills, but with no success. By posing as cat trappers, the stealthy duo gained access into the yards and homes of suspected moonshiners, getting close enough to smell the cooking alcohol.

They were not interested in trapping cats at all, something that would not have surprised Thoreau in the least.

The Problem with the Irish

In the years before the Civil War, Sandwich was known as a place where men liked to drink. Rightly or wrongly, the town had a reputation as the party capital of Cape Cod. Much of the intemperance was blamed on the Irish, who had been imported to work in the Boston and Sandwich Glass Company factory.

For a while, stories about the lengths men would go to get a drink were treated as humorous anecdotes. In 1848, the crew of the packet ship *Sarah* "borrowed" a bottled concoction from one of the passengers who had retired to his berth during a layover in Sandwich Harbor. The bottle was unmarked, but as men were well known to keep a flask close at hand for "medicinal" purposes, the *Sarah* crew was confident the bottle would cure what ailed them.

They all took turns sniffing the contents of the bottle to determine exactly what type of spirits they were holding. One man held the bottle under his nose, proclaimed it was gin and "nothing else," and took a deep swig. Another crewman snatched the bottle away and he, too, took a deep pull. Because of his haste, he missed the contorted face of the first man. The bottle, alas, contained the passenger's medicine, in which a powerful dose constituted only a few drops. The *Sarah* did not set sail the next day or for a few days thereafter, until the two crewmembers recovered from their indulgence of strong spirits.

Sandwich officials were not amused. At a town meeting in 1849, voters passed a bylaw that barred the sale of liquor except by the town-appointed liquor agent. Russell Lovell, in his book *Sandwich: A Cape Cod Town*, wrote that the agent could not sell his wares to drunkards and lawbreakers—the very persons who most desired alcohol and who, needless to say, would not let a little thing like a town bylaw keep them from getting it.

The longing for liquor was so strong in Sandwich that the town fathers were forced to use all means necessary to crack down on offenders. In the early 1850s, the legislature approved a state law that allowed authorities to search any home for liquor. Before being ruled unconstitutional in 1854, that law was invoked regularly in Sandwich, particularly in homes in the Irish section of town.

One particularly misguided fellow sent the following threatening letter to Capt. William Stutson, one of the instigators of the crackdown:

> *Captain Stutson*
> *we under stand that you are very bisey a bout*
> *other peopels bisnes and you had better look out*
> *for your self for if thare is not Rum a nuf to put*
> *out your Eyes there is vitrel a nuf and wee are*
> *deturmined that you shall have more fires to put*

*out this year than Rum shopes and your Hous
wod of ben Burnt Long agow if had not been for
god nobers and wee did not wish to dissterben
them and Frank Kerns had beter Lok for him
self for wee are determened to put a stopt to this
thing and wee dow not con sider it anew wors to
drink Rum than Chewing opeum and if you dow
not Look out for your self you will be sorry for
every Dolar that it Cost a Rum Sute it will
Cost you and your gang 10 this is from theme
that meenes it.*

Everyone's worst fears about rampant alcohol consumption were realized on Christmas Day 1857 when a group gathered at a Sandwich home for drinking and cardplaying. A man named McKune attempted to crash the party but was thrown out. He returned with several of his friends, who began tossing stones and sticks through the windows. One of the partiers inside the house loaded a shotgun and let loose a blast through one of the broken windows. The shot killed an innocent bystander, who had been watching the action from the street.

The death confirmed the dangers of demon rum. But it also confirmed that many of the town fathers had been mistaken about the source of the problem. It turned out that the "drunken shanty Irish" who owned the party house was named William Swift Jr., and the "besotted Irishman" who fired the fatal shot was named Charles Perry—Swift and Perry, family names that had been around Sandwich since the 1640s.

Likewise, the innocent victim who had been struck down in his prime was no *Mayflower* descendant, but instead a sober young man named Daniel Fogarty Jr.

A jury of his peers acquitted Perry of slaying the Irishman. With regards to the outcome, at least, some things never change.

The High Cost
of Missing Dinner

Gangster Al Capone met his downfall thanks to Elliot Ness and the Untouchables. John Dillinger had the Lady in the Red Dress. But for a Cape Cod bootlegging ring in 1925, it took an irate housewife from Brewster to trip them up.

It all started in late October when an unidentified shellfisherman from Brewster was slogging his way along the flats in Ellis Landing in search of some tasty clams. As he wandered near several cottages owned by George Hamblin, he was surprised to discover they were occupied.

While late October is beautiful on Cape Cod, it is not the type of weather that in those days attracted many tourists. And these off-season visitors were particularly ill tempered, as the shellfisherman was quick to learn. Three men approached and told him to find some other place to dig clams, as they had claim to the beach.

The shellfisherman returned home empty-handed. His wife, who apparently had planned on clams for dinner, was none too pleased at her husband's ill fortune. Like most native Cape Codders, she blamed her problem on the tourists and decided to retaliate by calling the authorities.

Cape police have no patience for rude tourists. When the shellfisherman's wife called, they quickly formed a "tourist welcoming committee" consisting of state and local police. These gentlemen armed themselves and drove out to Ellis Landing to teach the cottage dwellers some manners.

As the peace officers approached the cottage colony, several men inside one of the cottages made a break for it. They were persuaded to stop by Officer Bergstrom, who convinced them not so much with his words, but with the twelve-gauge shotgun he carried.

Police searched the cottage and found nothing. Two other cottages, however, contained all the provisions of these foul-tempered tourists—about $75,000 worth of Canadian whiskey and champagne.

No one in the group could explain the liquor. Police suspected that they were not planning a big party, possibly because possession of such large amounts of alcohol had been illegal since January 16, 1920, when the Eighteenth Amendment of the U.S. Constitution took effect.

In addition to the alcohol, police also found rifles with ammunition, binoculars for both day and night, and sounding lead, "the rope of which still was wet," according to a local newspaper. "There also were several blank checks drawn on a Jamaica Plain bank and the addresses of various trucking concerns."

The group of arrested "tourists" was so large that the police realized they needed larger transportation. They walked the prisoners to a nearby house whose owner had a school bus and chauffeured them to the Barnstable County Jail.

Being tourists, none of the men were from Cape Cod. They were identified as Fred Hartung and Ed Young of Fairhaven: Thomas Kelley and Harry Stevens of New Bedford; Charles

Earnest, William Hilton, and Joe Brennan of Boston; George Parker of Jamaica Plain; Byron Cassidy of Hyde Park; Walter Finn of Newton; and Hugh Simmons of Providence, Rhode Island.

At least one of them had some local connection, for he knew enough to call Wareham's crack Prohibition attorney, Frank Kiernan, who came down and bailed all the men out, at $200 each.

On that same day, the coast guard found an abandoned forty-foot motorboat anchored not far from a fish trap off East Brewster. On board, the coast guard discovered some 200 cases of champagne and whiskey. The owner of the boat was never found, possibly because he had been picked up in Ellis Landing earlier that day.

In total, authorities recovered around $100,000 in whiskey and champagne (and a boat) that day. All because a housewife in Brewster did not get clams for dinner.

Prohibition Ends with a Bang

President Herbert Hoover called it "the Noble Experiment." On the other hand, Hoover lost the 1932 presidential election by more than 7 million votes, a sure sign of how out of touch he had become.

Hoover's replacement, Franklin Delano Roosevelt, promised U.S. citizens a "New Deal." The American economy was in the midst of the Depression, and Roosevelt's vow brought renewed feelings of hope. Or maybe it was the promise that Roosevelt and Congress would repeal Hoover's "Noble Experiment," better known as Prohibition.

For thirteen years the Eighteenth Amendment to the U.S. Constitution had forbidden the manufacture of liquor, and the Volstead Act had made it illegal to buy it. By the time of Roosevelt's election in November 1932, the feds had made a half million arrests for violating Prohibition, which translated into 300,000 convictions. By Christmas 1932, the repeal of the Eighteenth Amendment was a certainty.

Cape Cod Confidential

Most Americans probably hoped that the end of Prohibition would also mean the end of the bootlegger. During the dry years, Cape Cod had become a major shipping port for illegal liquor. Barnstable County seemed to be overrun with professional gangsters, who allowed no one to interfere with their lucrative enterprise. In the mid-1920s, a Sandwich town official had tipped authorities to a big shipment coming on Cape. A few months later, that selectman, a former deputy sheriff, went out lobstering and disappeared. No one knew what happened to him until several weeks later when parts of his body began washing up on shore.

That was all coming to an end with the inevitable repeal of Prohibition. Time was running out, but at least in the mind of one Cape Cod man, opportunity remained for one final, big score.

Franklin Bearse lived with his wife and three children in Osterville. Throughout Prohibition he had been somewhat of a small-town celebrity. He pitched in the semipro New England Baseball League for the Lewiston team before returning to Barnstable County to play several years for Cape Cod Baseball League teams.

Somehow, in the early winter of 1932, Bearse learned of a garage overlooking Long Pond, right off Route 28 in Centerville, that was being used by bootleggers to store their illegal liquor. More importantly, Bearse knew that a couple of days before New Year's Day, the garage would be housing a truck filled with booze bound for Boston or Providence.

Bearse and six other Cape men decided to steal the truck. On the night of December 30, 1932, Bearse and the rest of the "gang" of hijackers climbed into a car driven Johnny Lewis, a young man barely out of his teens. Their plan, if it could be called that, was to force open the garage door and steal the booze-laden truck.

The garage was a huge building, big enough to hold two large trucks and all the cases of liquor they could carry. Once sealed, no light could escape from its windows or doors, enabling bootleggers to conduct their illegal activity at night and in private.

When Bearse and his cohorts opened the garage door, they found, as advertised, a truck filled with booze. But before they could start the truck, the hijackers were suddenly captured in the beams of several powerful spotlights.

The door to the garage was connected by electric circuit to a nearby cottage. When Bearse and his team opened the door, a bell rang in the cottage, which was filled with hardened men waiting for this very exigency.

Trapped in the spotlights, Bearse and the others were ordered to put up their hands. Instead they turned and ran for the woods. The spotlights followed them, making them easy targets for the bootleggers, who began shooting. Before Bearse made it halfway to the trees, he was dropped by a shotgun blast to the foot. As he fell, he took a .38 caliber slug in the back.

Two of the bootleggers grabbed the prone man and dragged him to the highway. There they found Johnny Lewis waiting behind the wheel of the getaway car. With a casualness that seemed to belie what had happened, the bootleggers threw Bearse's limp body into the car. "Take him to the hospital," one ordered Lewis. "And keep your mouth shut."

To hammer his point home, one of the men punched Lewis in the face. The blow broke a tooth. "And take that home with you," the bootlegger snarled.

Lewis did as he was told, but Bearse died before the car ever reached Cape Cod Hospital. The failed hijacker missed the New Year by only a few hours. Four months after his burial in Mosswood Cemetery in Cotuit, Prohibition was repealed.

There for the Taking

The Bible tells us not to covet the posses-
sions of others, but on Cape Cod there is a
long tradition of "borrowing" the belongings
of your neighbors. The tendency is so strong,
neither fish nor fowl are safe, and no church
sacred. As we shall learn, even the original
white settlers of this region, the Pilgrims,
were not immune. And if you can't trust a
Pilgrim, who can you trust?

The Berry Best Mother among the Pilgrims

Imagine this: Your husband's a layabout, your children are too young to be put to work, and you're a Pilgrim—what do you do? If your name happens to be Allice Berry and you live in Yarmouth some thirty years after the landing of the *Mayflower*, the answer is simple: you go on a crime spree.

You really couldn't blame her. Allice Berry's husband, Richard, was no damn good. In October 1649, Richard accused his friend, Teag Jones, of "having sodomy and other unclean practices with Sara, wife of Hugh Norman." The Plymouth General Court ordered Teag *and* Richard, along with two other men, held on a bond of £20 (about $5,000 today, an exorbitant sum). A few months later, Richard admitted he had made the whole thing up. For wasting the court's time, he was ordered whipped.

Eventually, Richard and Teag cleared up their little misunderstanding. That's when Allice's troubles really began. In

1653, Richard, being the lousy husband he was, forgot all about Mother's Day. Richard had a reasonable explanation for his absentmindedness, namely, that the holiday had not been invented. Still, he probably shuddered at the thought of coming home empty-handed to face his wife's eye rolling and her incessant muttering about "men and their lousy excuses." Coward that he was, he avoided the whole thing by moving in with Teag.

When Richard failed to come home, Allice certainly must have gone out to look for him, which could explain why she broke into her neighbors' houses. The frustration she felt at not finding her husband is probably what drove her to steal a neck cloth from one neighbor and some bacon and eggs from another.

A sympathetic Plymouth court resolved the problem by commanding Richard and Teag to cease their "uncivil living together." There is no record whether the court took action taken against Allice for her thievery. Allice and Richard must have patched things up, because she was soon pregnant with their second child.

The following year, with crime at an all-time high, the Plymouth General Court published a list of crimes for which the penalty was death. The court announced that a criminal could be hung for treason, murder, arson, sodomy, rape, and "buggery," which sounds really awful and was going on more than you might think. Having the Devil over for coffee and conversation also warranted a neck stretching. But the court offered some leniency with regard to theft. In Britain, they could hang you for stealing; the Pilgrim leaders instead required that the guilty party pay restitution "three or four fold according to the nature of the offense."

Having been made aware of the possible consequences of her actions, Allice Berry promptly went out and stole again. The following spring, she was brought up on charges of breaking into Benjamin Hammond's house and stealing an entire dress and a piece of pickled pork. The court records again mention no penalty, probably because Allice had discovered a loophole—you can't pay "three or four fold" if you have no money.

Three months later, Allice was at it again, this time charged with milking the Phelps family cow. For her udder lack of self-control, Allice was sentenced to pay ten shillings or spend an hour in the stocks. She undoubtedly chose the latter, and if so, she probably sat next to William Chase Jr., who had been convicted of breaking into the Berry house and "taking by violence" some flax and yarn. One suspects he had only been looking to recover some missing items from Mrs. Berry. They probably had a good laugh about it as they took their turns in the pillory.

That was the court's last dealing with Allice Berry. Richard, on the other hand, failed to reform. In 1663, he was caught playing cards and fined forty shillings. In 1668, he stole an axe. Finally in 1669, the court fined him five shillings for smoking in the Yarmouth Meeting House. He died in 1681. There is no record of Allice's death.

Despite what must have been a tumultuous home life, Allice's six children grew up and became productive citizens. Berrys can still be found throughout Cape Cod, and they and their ancestors have contributed to the well-being of this little peninsula. No mother could beg, borrow, or steal a better gift.

Fowl Deeds in
Barnstable County

C ape Cod is a natural poultry section," wrote E. E. Smith, secretary of the Cape Cod Poultry Association some eighty years ago. "Its well-drained soil is suitable for the production of home-grown feeds. The relatively mild, open winters permit free range, which produces vigorous stock; they also permit early hatching, which is conducive to egg production at the season of highest prices."

In 1910, for example, chickens outnumbered residents almost 4 to 1 (102,761 to 27,542). From those chickens, Cape Codders harvested almost 4 million eggs, amounting to a gross of eggs for every resident. Poultry in 1910 generated almost $200,000, and was second only to cranberries as an agricultural money crop. The value of fowl could not be overstated, and as such, chickens and other domestic birds became a favorite target of thieves.

Pilferage of these plumed animals was not tolerated. In the minds of some, stealing birds was a shooting offense. In 1857,

a gang of thieves broke into henhouses across Barnstable County. The *Yarmouth Register* printed a report of the pilferage, with the express purpose of putting the bandits on notice that "they are suspected and watched for," and the next time a hen roost is robbed, the reception they receive would not be so amenable. "If there is virtue in powder and shot, these miscreants will have it demonstrated upon themselves."

There seemed to be a direct correlation between chicken thefts and the national economy. During the depression of the 1890s, arrests for stealing chickens increased. And, perhaps in an attempt to kick-start the local economy, the courts spared no expense in bringing these thieves to justice.

Shortly before Christmas in 1892, George Ryder of Yarmouth was charged with stealing chickens from his neighbors. To prove his case, the local constable brought into court the evidence—namely, several cages of chickens that had been found on Ryder's property.

Ryder claimed that a friend had sold him the chickens. That friend came forward and on the witness stand corroborated Ryder's testimony, even pointing to one white, plain-looking hen that he claimed he recognized as one of the fowl he had sold.

When the trial resumed after lunch, the prosecution recalled Ryder's friend to the stand. In a tactic worthy of Perry Mason, the prosecutor removed the white hen from the cage and asked the witness to inspect it more closely, to be sure it was the right bird. The man studied the bird carefully and again confirmed that the chicken had been his, of that there was no mistake. The prosecutor then announced that the hen actually came from a farm near the courthouse, that he had switched them during the break. The judge sentenced Ryder to five months in the house of correction.

No less wily were chicken thieves themselves. In 1893, Charles Snow of Provincetown operated one of the largest chicken operations in town. One day, he and his son were checking their locked henhouse and were surprised to discover a group of boys inside robbing the roost. The gang ran for it, but Snow's son managed to catch two of their number after a short chase.

How had the boys managed to get inside a locked building? Apparently they had tunneled under a back wall. Had Snow and his son not happened upon the thieves, they could have made off with all the birds, and no one would have seen them.

Chickens were not the only birds prized by thieves. In 1882, a week or so before Thanksgiving, someone managed to steal all the pigeons in Orleans. An investigation turned up information that a gang from South Yarmouth had sneaked into town and robbed the roosts.

Two of the victims, W. M. Crosby and J. E. Taylor, met one of the suspects at his home in South Yarmouth and innocently asked if he had any pigeons for sale. The suspect claimed he owned no pigeons, and furthermore that he didn't want any.

Then the man's mother came out and told the two Orleans men the same. Their veracity immediately came into question when Crosby pointed out a cage full of fantail pigeons that looked very much like the ones taken from his house. As luck would have it, Deputy Sheriff Matthews of Yarmouth showed up about that time. A search of the neighborhood turned up almost every pigeon that had been stolen.

Pigeons as food fell out of fashion by the twentieth century, but there were still some traditionalists who could not give up the old ways. One was David Sears of Dennisport, accused of pilfering pigeons in 1939. Sears, police said, stole the pigeons while on an errand of mercy. A friend had taken ill, and a doctor had prescribed chicken broth. Sears broke into a neighbor's henhouse at night and stole four pet pigeons, which he gave to his friend. Police tracked down the culprit by following a trail of pigeon feathers.

A few months later, authorities managed to flush out another pigeon thief. In May that year, one of Oscar Snow's

prized carrier pigeons mysteriously returned to his coop at the Nauset coast guard station after an absence of almost a year. Snow suspected his pigeon had been birdnapped by another pigeon fancier, John Correiro of Provincetown. To prove his theory, Snow drove out to Correiro's home and hid nearby, where he had a clear view of Correiro's pigeon coop. Back at his house, Snow's wife frightened the pigeons into flight. Sure enough, Snow watched as his prized pigeon flew into Correiro's coop.

Snow went to court and got a warrant. In the company of a Provincetown police officer, he searched Correiro's coop and found his bird. Some of its feathers had recently been pulled so it couldn't fly.

Correiro pleaded not guilty to larceny, but a judge disagreed and ordered the man to pay Snow restitution in the amount of $3.

Caught by the Organ

Wellfleet was in the midst of a crime wave, or, at least, what passed for a crime wave in the fall of 1872. Someone stole three barrels of Isaac Hatch's finest cranberries. The thief also made off with several lengths of rope, a harness, and a wooden block and tackle. Down in Wellfleet Harbor, authorities believed the same party lifted some $50 in clothing, enough to dress a dozen men, from several ships docked at the wharf. A small dory also went missing, probably used to transport the loot out of Wellfleet.

When the members of the Congregational Society filed into the church on Main Street that Sunday for their weekly dose of worship, they discovered more evidence of the crime wave. When A. J. Smith, the organist, sat down to play, there was an empty space where his fingers were supposed to go. The organ was gone, and although that was not a normal occurrence, Mr. Smith assumed someone during the week had

removed it to be repaired in Boston. The organ was somewhat old and was due to be replaced. Still, it struck him as unusual that no one had bothered to mention it to him.

The choir went ahead a cappella, and the parishioners sang their songs to the Lord probably more off-key than usual.

It had occurred to no one until after the Sunday service that the organ had been stolen. There were no clues as to who had taken it or when. Certainly the theft was connected to the missing cranberries, equipment, and clothing.

Several days later in East Dennis, a man named Joseph Brown walked aboard the *David Porter*, a packet ship, and queried Capt. Orrin Sears about some furniture he wished moved from South Wellfleet to Boston. After negotiating a fee, the men agreed they would set sail on Thursday.

In due time, Brown rowed up to the *David Porter* in a dory, which was laden with four barrels and a giant ice chest. The cargo was soon stowed aboard with the other goods bound for Boston. The departure, unfortunately, had to be delayed due to inclement weather, and Captain Sears made plans to depart the following week.

When Saturday arrived, so did Captain Sears' copy of the local newspaper. In the Wellfleet column was a piece about the missing cranberries and the theft of the organ. Later in the day, Captain Sears found himself in conversation with Stillman Kelley and Nathan Sears, owners of an East Dennis fish house. They told him that they believed someone had been on their property and stolen some fish.

As is natural to all Cape Codders, their suspicions immediately fell upon the stranger Brown. They learned he had sold his dory to a party in Dennis for $1, a ridiculous sum. The three men wired the constables in Wellfleet, who came down on the first train Monday. Upon arrival, they cracked open the ice chest and discovered it stuffed with clothes, not ice. The chest's weight belied there was more inside than just clothing, and after peeling away the layers of trousers, shirts, and jackets, there was the missing Wellfleet church organ.

Arrested and grilled for the names of his accomplices, Brown admitted to the theft, but declined to name anyone who may have assisted him. It is possible he had no help. Any man who can row a dory loaded with an organ and three barrels of cranberries from Wellfleet to Dennis could certainly manhandle an organ using a block and tackle.

The following year, Brown went to trial, where he pleaded guilty. On three counts of breaking and entering, for the three barrels of cranberries, he received two years each. For stealing the organ, he received six months at hard labor in the New Bedford House of Correction. One suspects that any man who can row a church organ over eight miles of open water would not find "hard labor" in prison too taxing.

The Crime Wave
of 1878

L ike most small, insular communities, Cape Codders of
  old held a particular dislike and fear of strangers. Paying
  tourists, even as far back as colonial times, were tolerated, and in some cases even appreciated; those who came to the
Cape with more shaky finances were scourges to be dealt with
in the most blunt and direct manner.

Cape Cod has always had a population of tramps,
so-called. The climate makes it possible to spend a winter out
of doors. It is close enough to the Athens of America, Boston,
that those who exhaust their funds on the sins of the city could
scrape together enough train fare to beg it out on Cape Cod.

When the Industrial Revolution broke out across the
country in the 1800s, Americans began to hit the road in
search of work and opportunity. The homeless suddenly
invaded Cape Cod.

In late 1878, Dennis found itself in the grips of a crime
wave. Over the course of a month, thirteen homes were broken
into; all the break-ins were blamed on tramps.

The crime spree began at Jonathan Bangs's house. Burglars sprang the bolts to the kitchen door and made off with milk, pie, cake, and apples. They then moved to Mrs. Lothrop Thacher's house, forcing a window and making off with mince pies, bread, and cake.

Charlie Underwood's home was next—this time they took cornmeal. His neighbor, Capt. George Thacher, lost enough food to last a thief for several days.

A few days later, on November 15, Capt. Obed Baker II, Dennis town clerk, found his home had been broken into and a supply of fresh milk taken. On November 18, the break-in artists forced their way into the Reverend Alpheus Nickerson's home, where they swiped bread and cake, and knocked a hole in his flour barrel.

That same night, someone scaled a piazza and broke a pane of glass in a window to get into Mrs. J. L. Baxter's house. Mrs. Baxter surprised the burglars, who jumped out the window and vaulted the porch.

What every tramp wants is a home to call their own; if none exists, then they borrow somebody else's. The thieves apparently found Capt. Freeman Gage's home in South Dennis empty, so they invited themselves inside and spent several days enjoying the hospitality. When the captain did return, he found the remains of several meals, many made with food-stuffs taken from his neighbors. One bed was ruined, although news reports at the time did not specify how. No silver or other valuable was missing, save for a quilt, a blanket, six sheets, one of the captain's new flannel shirts, and some tins of beef.

At Captain William Evans's home, the thieves borrowed a rubber coat and a pair of rubber boots. On December 8, the transients broke into Mrs. B. D. Overton's house and made off with pies, cake, and bread, as well as a knife with which to properly serve their victuals. A week later, they were in Mary Nickerson's house. Apparently, they did not cotton to her cooking and instead stole a gold locket that contained photos of her two sons, Boston lawyer Joseph Nickerson and the Reverend Alpheus Nickerson, whose home the thieves had visited the previous month. They also stole a string of gold beads and a glass lamp. Two days later, the gold beads were found wound around the doorknob of the Reverend Nickerson's home, probably as payment so that the good minister could repair his flour barrel.

The gang broke into Capt. Charles Emery's house, taking two comforters and some alcohol. They had even taken the trouble to light a lamp to see what there was to steal. The lamp's chimney was broken, and the room was filled with smoke, ruining whatever the thieves had not taken. Later the next day, the tramps returned and stole some cotton wool and foodstuffs. Also later that day, a man wearing rubber boots and a slouch hat (the former, no doubt, the spoils from Captain Evans's house; no word on where the vagrant had acquired the latter) tried to remove a key from inside the door of Capt. Roland Kelley's house. The vagrant fled before he could be captured. The next day, thieves visited Capt. Lorenzo Chase's home, stealing a new ulster coat and all the food in the house.

For some reason, the tramps left South Dennis and went to try their luck in West Dennis. There they found the hospitality

somewhat less inviting. On December 14, Capt. Van Buren Chase was in the middle of his supper when he looked up to see someone peering in his window. Firearm ready, the captain went to the door and squeezed off a shot, but the tramp was gone.

Capt. Aberdeen Child was also eating his supper that night when he heard a noise in his kitchen. He found a tramp standing by his stove. The captain asked the man why he was there. "To warm myself and get something to eat," the man replied. Instead of going to pantry to feed his guest, Captain Child went looking for his pistol. The tramp took to his heels, but did not get out of sight before the good captain could get off a round or two.

A few days before Christmas, the daughter of Capt. Samuel Small caught a glimpse of a tramp outside a window. She opened the door and invited the man in, telling him everyone was at home. The tramp took off, and Captain Small went after him with a rifle, but lost him in the woods.

As the definition of "Christian charity" in West Dennis did not include the feeding and clothing of the homeless, the tramps found somewhere else to roam. The crime wave came to an abrupt end.

The Shell Game

In the 1800s, the lure of gold in the hills of California enticed many a Cape Cod man. Those were the dumb ones. Many a fortune has been found in Cape Cod's sands. Gold has another name in these parts—it's called "shellfish."

Harvesting shellfish is a lot simpler than digging for gold, especially once you get the hang of it. The tools of the trade are easily obtained—clam and quahog rakes, a basket or bucket (better yet, a "dreener"). The truly indigent can eschew any tools and instead walk out on the mudflats and pick them up with their bare hands.

Even though the shellfish are pretty much lying around for anyone to gather, there have always been unscrupulous persons who would rather steal someone else's catch than put a foot in the muck to get their own. Heck, there are probably people who would be willing to steal dirt if you put a price on it.

Pilfering someone's dinner is one thing, but pilfering one's livelihood is a whole different kettle of fish. Commercial shellfishing is backbreaking work, and the fruits of that labor have long been the target of thieves. So much so that the craving of someone else's shellfish probably should be considered the eighth deadly sin, at least on Cape Cod anyway.

While there is certainly thievery of commercial shellfish today, in the nineteenth century it was big news. Few Cape Cod newspapers wasted any ink on the White Chapel murders (perpetrated by a gent known as Jack the Ripper), but the theft of a single scallop was enough to remake page one or even put out an extra edition.

In those days there were three ways to steal commercial shellfish. One could dig up another man's shellfish beds. Oysters, for example, are frequently cultivated in shallow sea beds. Shellfish thieves are particularly fond of these "oyster grants," as they are called, for they eliminate having to search through a lot of mud to find shellfish.

To avoid heavy predation of their shellfish beds, fishermen will usually team up and form a saltwater version of a neighborhood watch. In May 1881, several oyster-grant holders in Wareham managed to capture a shellfish thief who had been raiding their oyster beds for months. The man was from Agawam, which supposedly was "the home of several other of... a class of people who are as obnoxious to our community as the meanest dog that was ever given birth," according to a local newspaper at the time. "They steal from each other and too, before our courts, commit perjury after perjury. When they cannot find oyster grants to rob, they, on dark nights, visit our iron establishments and from them steal what loose iron they can see and take out of town." One hopes the newspaper editor did not serve on that thief's jury.

The second way to steal shellfish in the 1800s was to poach them out of season. Normally this is illegal, but in the late 1890s a group of fishermen in Chatham found a loophole. Fishing regulations at the time forbade the harvest of scallops using nets. There was nothing, however, to forbid anyone from using his or her hands. Scallops back then were so plentiful that anyone could walk out onto the mudflats as the tide receded and collect a basketful. In the month before the opening of scallop season, a group of fishermen began harvesting scallops by hand, opening them and salting them down. On the day the season opened, they washed the catch in fresh water to revive it, and shipped it to the Boston fish market, where it fetched top prices. This scam worked until the legislature changed the law.

The third and best way to steal shellfish was to heist the crop after harvesting. For three straight years in the late 1880s, someone stole hundreds of pounds of shucked scallops from the freight yard in Hyannis. The railroad tried everything to protect the cargo, even hiring armed guards as night watchmen, but the thief or thieves, like the shellfish they stole, proved too slippery.

As is the usual case, the culprit was caught by accident. One cold night in December 1889, Police Officer John Bearse was on his way to a lodge meeting when he decided, on a whim, to leave his horse and wagon in a shed next to his friend's grain store, which was next to the railroad depot. As he was leaving the shed, Officer Bearse by chance passed his lantern over a tub that sat next to the grain store and looked out of place. Curious, he went over and found that the tub was full of shucked scallops. The container had no identifying card, and Officer Bearse surmised right away that it had been stolen. He woke the station agent, who lived nearby, and the two men set a watch on the tub to see who would claim it.

They did not have long to wait. A slovenly dressed man soon appeared to take the tub of scallops and carry them into a nearby field. He returned with a wheelbarrow, into which he loaded the scallops.

The night was dark, and neither Officer Bearse nor the station agent could make out the features of their culprit. Their quarry, however, soon accommodated them by wheeling his stolen goods under a streetlight close to where the two men were hiding. Officer Bearse instantly recognized the thief as a local man named Edwin Kelley.

The two men stepped into the light and confronted Kelley, who, according to a local newspaper, "dropped the wheelbarrow and fainted away."

The Postmaster Who Delivered
One Letter too Many

Someone had robbed the Falmouth National Bank without having to blow the safe or hold a teller at gunpoint. The villain did not even so much as walk in the door, but managed to abscond with $500 of the bank's money.

A few months before the first shot at Fort Sumter started the Civil War, postal authorities received a report that someone had stolen $500 from a mail pouch belonging to the Falmouth bank. Authorities believed it had to be a conspiracy—the Parker gang from Bourne.

Well, not a gang really. Erastus Parker was postmaster and stationmaster at what is today Monument Beach in Bourne. His son-in-law, Joseph Hewins, and Joseph's brother, Henry, drove the stagecoach between Bourne and Woods Hole.

Postal investigators immediately suspected the theft had been an inside job, not an unusual circumstance in the middle part of the nineteenth century. Every year, the Secret Service of

the Post Office Department arrested almost 200 postal employees for stealing everything from stamps to postal receipts to money transported through the mail. What brought suspicion on Parker and his kin is not known.

The case took more than a year to investigate, but on June 1862, Parker and the two Hewins brothers stood trial in Boston. The Hewinses faced five different counts. Authorities must have suspected Parker to be the ringleader, for he faced seven.

Prosecuting Parker was none other than Richard Henry Dana Jr., a man for whom it might be argued the United States was fighting a civil war in the first place. While Dana was no Abolitionist, he did defend a couple of fugitive slaves, Anthony Burns and Shadrach Minkins, who had been captured in Boston and, under the Fugitive Slave Law, faced return to their slave masters in the South. When Dana's legal acumen proved to be insufficient to win the freedom of either man, Dana's accomplices found other ways to manumit the two slaves. They purchased Shadrach Minkins from his owner and spirited Anthony Burns to Canada after a group of men raided the courthouse in Boston and broke him out.

Before becoming a lawyer, Dana had been a best-selling author. His book, *Two Years Before the Mast*, was an immensely popular account of his sea voyage to pre-Gold Rush California. Dana was particularly fond of sailors and the maritime industry, but apparently that fondness did not include a crusty old Cape Codder like Erastus Parker. Dana prosecuted Parker with great relish.

Sadly, details of the trial have been lost to the mists of time. In 1862, newspapers at the time were more occupied with news from the war front than the federal courts. The Parker trial warranted only a paragraph or two.

One witness to the trial, a friend of Parker's and therefore less than impartial, later described it as possessing "the extraordinary rulings of the court, the rejection and suppression of important evidence for the accused, the expart combinations forestalling judgment, the earnest persistency of the District Attorney, and the unseemly haste and abruptness with which the trial was brought to a close."

The Hewins brothers escaped conviction. Parker was not as lucky. When the jury returned with its verdict, these twelve men decided that the prosecution failed to prove that Parker stole the letter or opened the letter or removed the $500. With the acquittal of the Hewins brothers, the government could not prove there was any conspiracy. The only count the jury agreed upon was the last—"receiving and concealing a banknote that had been stolen from the mails."

In the eyes of one observer, all the prosecution could prove was that the money had passed through Parker's hands—something he could not avoid in his role as postmaster. Because somebody had to steal the money, the jury accepted the argument of the U.S. attorney and convicted Parker.

The sanctity of the post office requires that its employees have the highest integrity. Even though convicted on only one count, that sole charge carried with it a stiff penalty for Parker. The federal judge sentenced Parker to five years hard labor to be served at the Plymouth House of Correction. Parker's lawyers attempted an appeal, but Dana saw to it that the conviction stuck.

In late October 1866, President Andrew Johnson pardoned Parker, an action that had been "recommended by many influential citizens." Many of those citizens turned out a week after Parker arrived home for a special celebration. The pardon, however, did not overturn the conviction. Parker was a convicted thief, one who in the eyes of the law had stolen $500 from the U.S. Mails. What kind of job could Parker expect to get after having been convicted of violating that most sacred of public institutions, the U.S. Postal Service?

There was no reason to worry about Erastus Parker. He had no trouble finding a job—as postmaster at Monument Beach, a position he returned to and served in for another six years.

Assault & Battery

Settling one's differences with fisticuffs may not seem very civilized, but no one has ever accused Cape Cod of civility. In a locale where families go back to the Mayflower, one clan can hold a grudge against another for decades. Every few generations, there comes a time when scores must be settled. The one stabilizing force on the Cape has been the church, but sometimes, as we shall learn, hands are not always clasped in prayer.

You Can Call Me "Captain"

If you had suddenly landed on Cape Cod in the 1800s, you would swear that every man went by the title of "Captain." Anyone who skippered anything from a three-masted schooner to a harbor dinghy qualified. One can imagine visiting the village post office in the nineteenth century and finding the air filled with greetings of "Morning, Captain," "How are you today, Cap'n," "You're looking well, Captain."

As shipping faded, these seafaring men moved ashore, took up residence on Cape Cod, and grew older. They sometimes forgot that they were no longer masters of their vessel.

Such was the case one blustery spring day in 1857, when Capt. Frances Small and Capt. Edward Crowell, both of West Dennis and both seventy, were disagreeing over a piece of fence. The men had known each other almost their entire lives. Captain Small and Captain Crowell were related by marriage; the former had married a Crowell.

The two men met by a pond and commenced to argue. Harrison G. Alexander happened to be working on a house nearby. "I heard someone say, 'You're a liar,'" he recalled later. Captain Small, who had an injured leg and relied on a cane to get around, could be seen holding it in a threatening manner.

Alexander possessed a trait common to Cape Codders, and that was he knew when to mind his own business. He went into the house for a few minutes, and when he came back out, Captain Small was standing in the water, his clothes soaked, and he appeared to be fishing out his hat, which was floating toward him. Captain Crowell stood on the shore, holding Captain Small's cane and apparently not offering to help its owner out of the drink.

Once he recovered his hat, Captain Small grabbed his cane and squished his way home. Captain Crowell, blood on his face, went over to Alexander and explained, "The old rebel struck me, and I put him under water. Have got too much of the old Crowell blood to be struck by a Small."

By the time Captain Small got home, he was pale, trembling, and complaining of pain in his stomach. He changed out of his wet clothes and had several strong drinks, but he could not seem to warm. He shivered all night. The next morning he tried to get up and promptly fell on the floor senseless.

Captain Small's physician, Dr. Hurlburt, found his patient in bed, his body temperature low and with an almost imperceptible pulse. Captain Small also could not talk. The doctor prescribed opium and brandy every half hour until his system returned.

Word spread around the village that Captain Small was in bad shape. Captain Crowell was visiting a friend and his nephew James Small, who also was a nephew to Captain Small. "Uncle Edward, how could you put Uncle Francis into the water, and hold him under until the bubbles rose?" James Small asked. "I did not drag him into the water," Captain Crowell said angrily, according to one account. "He called me a thief and struck me on the head, and in the scuffle, I held him into the water. Either of you would do the same in self-defense."

Another version of the same conversation cited his reply as, "I didn't drag him in, but pushed him in, and would do so again under the circumstances, and so would either of you."

Two days later, Captain Small was dead. A Barnstable grand jury indicted the aged Captain Crowell on charges of manslaughter.

When Captain Crowell went to trial, he was unrepentant. He fortunately drew a jury of his peers: all were male, all were Cape Codders, and more than one would have answered if you called him "Captain." The verdict, predictably, was not guilty.

Murderous Methodists
Of Harwich

In August 1892, some deranged person tried to kill the Methodist minister of Harwich. The Reverend David Chambers, who had been preaching in town for only a few months, was returning to his boardinghouse just across the town line in Chatham after spending an evening with several young men and women of East Harwich when he was struck in the back of the neck with a three-pound rock.

The woman who owned the boardinghouse, Zebina Chase, had heard the reverend on the porch and was about to let him in when the door burst open and the young man fell into her arms unconscious.

Mrs. Chase called for her daughter, and the two managed to drag the unconscious man into a chair. She ran to the front door and shouted for her neighbors. "Come here!" she cried. "Somebody has killed the minister!"

Isaac Kendrick and his son answered her call and sent for the doctor. Dr. Patterson of Harwich arrived in about an hour.

The unfortunate divine then began to regain consciousness and his first words were, "It's too bad that I should suffer for what other people have done."

Mr. Kendrick went outside with a lantern and found the weapon—a flat stone, weighing three pounds. The Reverend Chambers had received but a glancing blow, for the full force of the stone upon his head would have split his head like a melon. Dr. Ball of Boston happened to be summering in the area, and after an examination of the reverend, he concurred. "The pastor narrowly escaped concussion of the brain, which would have been the result if it had struck him an inch higher," he said later. The Reverend Chambers would recover, he decided.

Authorities later learned the minister had been receiving threats against his life in the mail for several weeks. On July 5, the Reverend Chambers found in his mail a letter postmarked two days before from Fremont, Nebraska. Inside was a note, written in a disguised hand, ordering him to leave town or be killed. His boardinghouse, the letter said, was a "house of assignation" (read: house of ill repute), and his wife would be regarded a whore if she remained. The reverend destroyed the letter, but kept the envelope, and promptly forgot about the whole incident.

A week before the attack, he received another one, again postmarked from Nebraska. This letter gave him twenty-four hours' notice to leave town and said, "If you don't get out, you will be helped out." He again destroyed the communication, but did mention it to some friends, cautioning them not to make it public as he did not wish to arouse any feeling over the matter.

A few hours before the assault, the Reverend Chambers had received another letter in the same disguised handwriting. This one had been mailed from Harwich, on Cape Cod, and inside it read: "Chambers—If you have received a previous letter of warning you must be guided by it or take the consequences. This is final."

That evening, on his way to the post office to mail some letters, he met a daughter of Mr. Kendrick, who invited him to spend the evening at her house with some friends.

As the two of them walked along a path, Miss Kendrick saw a man hiding in the corn nearby. Rev. Chambers, who was hard of hearing, gave no sign of noticing him, and she did not mention it. At 9:30, some young men going down the street noticed a man skulking about the corn.

The Reverend Chambers, after accompanying some ladies home to the next house, crossed the street to his boarding place at about 9:45 and, passing in by the front of the house, went around to the door. It was dark under the trees and as he reached out to grasp the knob he heard footsteps close behind him and partly turned toward the street. Suddenly he felt something strike him on the back of his neck and that was the last he knew for hours.

Immediately following the assault, the talk of the town was that Rev. Chambers was being punished by those who would like to keep the Methodist church in town split. Two years before, the Methodist community in Harwich divided over a scandal: Deacon Jonathan Buck had been seeking the affections of another deacon's wife. The Reverend Chambers, in the relatively short time he had been preaching in Harwich, had brought many of the Harwich Methodists back under one roof.

The Reverend Chambers recovered from the attack and continued to spread the Gospel undeterred in Harwich for several months. But on Valentine's Day the following year, someone threw another large stone at him as he was leaving his boardinghouse that evening. It narrowly missed his head and crashed through a nearby window.

Once again, the good reverend had received a missive before the attack, this time a postcard that read: "Come to the South Harwich depot at 8 o'clock alone." He was on his way to that appointment when attacked.

Mr. Chambers continued his ministry for three more weeks, but on Sunday, March 11, he disappeared. He turned up the next day, packed up his belongings and left town.

It was shortly after his departure that the truth came out. Rev. Chambers's problems had nothing and everything to do with the scandal in Harwich two years before; Rev. Chambers was not being punished for the sins of Deacon Buck, he was duplicating them.

As Mrs. Norton Steele told a reporter from the *Boston Herald* the day the reverend left town, she had been a victim of his desires. She had hired him to teach her daughter to paint. "One day after he had finished his work we stood in the dining room, and were speaking of the rapid advancement my daughter was making, when he crossed the room to where I was and attempted to embrace and kiss me," she said. "I held him off, however, and ordered him out. 'There is the door,' I said, 'and don't darken it again.'"

It appeared that the actions of the reverend in Mrs. Stone's story had been repeated throughout the area. The last straw had been the reverend's conduct following a church fundraiser. The ladies of the church offered a few hours of their attention at auction, and Rev. Chambers was the successful bidder for the attentions of a married woman from South Chatham who could only be described as beautiful.

Following the sale, the good reverend's behavior with the woman displayed his intention to get his money's worth, and the wife fled the minister to tell her husband of his overtures.

A postscript to the tale of Mr. Chambers: he sued the *Herald* and five other newspapers for libel. He never collected a dime. As they say in the biz, the story stands.

The Sour History of the Sweet Science

The Sour History of the Sweet Science

Boxing is called the sweet science, but on Cape Cod, the history of the brawl has been less a matter for the academy and more a matter for the judicial system.

The conflict over boxing and wrestling was evident from the very first years of white settlement. The bluenoses who settled New England believed that having organized fun was a sin. From the start, the colonists found themselves in conflict over those who worked and those who worked at sports.

Governor William Bradford, who came over on the *Mayflower*, took a particularly dim view of what today are cultural centerpieces of America—sports and Christmas. As he wrote in his journal:

> On the day called Christmas, the Governor called
> the people out to work, but most of this new com-
> pany [recently arrived on the ship *Fortune*]
> excused themselves and said it went against their

consciences to work on this day. So the Governor told them that if they made it a matter of conscience, he would spare them till they were better informed. When [Bradford] *came home at noon from work, he found them in the street at play; some pitching the barr* [throwing weights] *and some at stoole-ball* [an early form of cricket], *and such like sports. So he went to them and took away their implements and told them what they were doing was against his conscience, that they should play while others worked. If they made the keeping of Christmas a matter of devotion, he said, then let them stay in their houses, but there should be no gaming or reveling in the streets. Since which time nothing hath been attempted that way, at least openly.*

Governor Bradford was dead only three years when history records the first open violation of his "no games on Christmas" decree. It happened on Cape Cod, away from the prying eyes of Plymouth.

On Christmas Day in 1660, two men from different towns met to do battle the old-fashioned way, with their bare hands. In one corner was Joseph Rogers of Eastham; in the other, John Hawes of Yarmouth. Rogers was the grandson of one of the original Pilgrims (or Saints, as they liked to call themselves), Thomas Rogers. The Hawes name does not appear on the *Mayflower* register, so perhaps he was one of those washashores who constituted a group sometimes referred to as "Strangers."

The only account of this battle between Saint and Stranger appears in the court order records of the Plymouth colony. At some point during their manly struggle, Hawes, "violently and by force of armes," apparently smashed Rogers to the ground. As far as the wrestling match was concerned, Hawes proved to be the winner because Rogers did not get up. As far as the grand jury was concerned, it was not so much wrestling as it was murder, for Rogers lingered for two days then died. The grand jury ruled that Hawes should stand trial for murder for "takeing away the life of Josephth Rogers of Eastham by giving him a most deadly fall."

Apparently Hawes drew some sports fans on his jury, for that spring he was found not guilty. Even though Hawes was a free man, those who desired to pursue the manly arts would find only persecution for centuries to come.

Even as late as the 1890s, society banned friendly wagers on the outcome of two men pounding themselves senseless. In 1893, a group of Lower Cape men conspired to bring a professional boxing match to the Cape. The men had arranged to return hometown champ Ellwood Rogers (no doubt a descendant of the late Joseph Rogers) from his gym in Boston to face a man so terrible he went by only one name—"Donald," although whether that was his first or last name remains a mystery. The two men had sparred once before, and Donald had been the victor. This time, fighting on his home turf, Rogers figured to restore his honor.

Fight fans looked forward to the bout on March 22 at the Society Hall in East Harwich. Every precaution had been taken to keep the match a secret, for the authorities frowned on prizefighting, but someone had the bright idea to sell tickets for the event. Although there was no such thing as 911 or a police radio, there was the telegraph, and police from all over the Cape managed to get word there was to be a raid in East Harwich.

It is not known how many of the $2 or $3 tickets were sold, but when police raided the hall on the night of the fight, there were only thirty-two men inside. Supposedly several of the ticket holders had gotten wind that the jig was up, hence the poor turnout. Considering the purse for the fight was $800, it looked as if the night was going to be a loss for the promoters, so perhaps they were actually the ones who had contacted the authorities.

Rogers was already stripped to the waist when the local police wandered in. Upon seeing them, he walked to the center of the ring, and announced, "Gentlemen, owing to the weather and circumstances, this thing will have to be postponed."

Police apparently made no arrests. Outside the hall, Rogers graciously gave Donald $100 for his troubles, but then promised him they would meet again and it would be on the Cape. There is no record as to whether the fight occurred; if it did, at least this time they managed to keep it secret.

In Defense of
Anthony Johnson

In Defense of
Anthony Johnson

D eputy Sheriff Ezra Pope of Sandwich had his orders. He was to arrest Anthony Johnson for breaking into the house of a neighbor, William Mountley.

Breaking and entering was a fairly serious crime in 1863. Most of the able-bodied men on the Cape were away defending the Union in the Civil War, leaving behind women and children, the old and infirm. Busting into a man's house while he was away fighting a war was considered tantamount to treason.

If Pope did not know Anthony Johnson (which was unlikely, as they lived in the same town), the deputy sheriff would have no trouble identifying him. Johnson was an African American—"colored," as the local papers described him.

Deputy Sheriff Pope found Johnson at or near his home in what is today the Sagamore section of Bourne. Johnson, from all accounts, declined Deputy Sheriff Pope's offer of free room and board in the county lockup in the most impolite fashion:

he picked up his shotgun and let loose a round in the general direction of the lawman.

A shotgun blast at close range can cut a man in half. Fortunately, Deputy Sheriff Pope had not approached his quarry too closely. He was hit with only three pieces of buckshot, which barely broke the skin. Rather than persist in his attempt to arrest Johnson, the deputy sheriff decided to return home and wait for the court to issue a new warrant, this time for resisting arrest and assault upon an officer of the law.

Johnson showed up for his trial in Barnstable Superior Court in April of 1864, but he did not come alone. He brought a lawyer. While today it is considered the right of every defendant to have legal counsel, this was not necessarily the norm in the 1800s. If the charge was serious enough, such as murder, the court would make sure that the defendant had representation. But for most crimes, only those who could afford them employed lawyers.

Not only did Anthony Johnson have a lawyer, but he had a good one. The newspapers made note of his defense attorney's abilities, how he defended Johnson "with a good deal of shrewdness and zeal." Clearly Johnson's lawyer was something special, the type of high-powered defense attorney not normally seen around these parts.

Indeed, Johnson's lawyer was even more special than that. For like Johnson, he was an African American. Although the newspapers did not say it, he was one of the first African American lawyers in the United States.

William Henry Johnson was his name. He had been born a slave in Virginia and had ended up in New Bedford before the Civil War. While he might have been related to his client, there was an even better chance that he wasn't. It turned out the name Johnson "had been assumed by nearly every slave who arrived in New Bedford" as part of the Underground Railroad, according to an escaped slave named Frederick

Johnson who, to avoid confusion with the New Bedford Johnsons, changed his name to Frederick Douglass.

New Bedford in the years before the Civil War was a sanctuary for escaped slaves, according to Douglass. Shortly after arriving in the city, Douglass learned that "there was nothing in the constitution of Massachusetts to prevent a colored man from holding any office in the state. There in New Bedford the black man's children ... went to school side by side with the white children, and apparently without objection from any quarter."

More importantly, there were jobs in New Bedford. William Henry Johnson found employment as a janitor in a small law office. While there, he "became interested in reading law books." That was the only legal education he received.

When he defended Anthony Johnson in Barnstable Superior Court in April of 1864, the black man was not even a member of the Massachusetts Bar. This may have been one of his very first cases. Only eighteen months before, slavery was still legal in the United States, and if William Henry Johnson was a runaway, he could have been captured and returned to the South. In September 1862, Abraham Lincoln signed the Emancipation Proclamation, and surely William Henry Johnson would have felt safe to practice his craft openly by that time.

Accepted to the Massachusetts Bar within days of the end of the Civil War in 1865, William Henry Johnson became one of a half dozen African American lawyers in the entire United States. He became the first African American lawyer to try cases in New Hampshire and Rhode Island. He went on to become an expert in administrative law and built up a considerable practice defending men and women accused of violating liquor laws. Johnson himself was a teetotaler, and was one of the leaders of New Bedford's temperance movement. He was so respected for his abilities that he won election to a term on the New Bedford Common Council in 1880. He died in 1895.

More than thirty years before his death, he used every lawyerly trick he knew to win acquittal for Anthony Johnson. While the Barnstable court and local press were impressed with William Henry Johnson's legal acumen, it was not enough to save his client. The jury found Anthony Johnson guilty and sentenced him to a year in the house of correction, a seemingly light sentence when one considers he shot a police officer.

When Anthony Johnson walked out of the house of correction, the Civil War was over. Like four million of his brothers and sisters in the South, he was a free man.

Not So Innocent until Proven Guilty

So what does a guy have to do to get fired around here?"

There is a perception that the world today is going to hell in a handbasket because employers can no longer fire people like they used to. A mountain of red tape protects employees, we are told, and only the grossest misconduct is legitimate grounds to dismiss them.

That must have been what Cape Codders a century ago thought when they learned of the case of the Reverend Delbert C. Donnocker.

In August 1893, the combined school committees of Mashpee, Sandwich, and Bourne elected the Reverend Donnocker to the post of superintendent. The vote had not been unanimous and had split along town lines: Mashpee and Bourne wanted Donnocker, and Sandwich adamantly did not.

Bourne and Sandwich in 1893 were engaged in a dispute, the details of which were never described. Perhaps it was simply the rebellion of a child against its parent, for Bourne had split off from Sandwich only nine years before to form its own town. It appears pretty clear that the Reverend Donnocker was selected as superintendent out of spite, although no one, not even the Sandwich School Committee, disputed the Baptist minister's qualifications.

Credit Sandwich's reluctance to rumors that the minister had been involved in some—ahem—shenanigans at one of his last assignments at the Free Will Baptist Church in Scarboro, Maine. Members of the Bourne committee had heard the same rumors, but did not feel they were of enough gravity to withhold the job. Sandwich's convictions that Donnocker was the wrong man were so strong that, after he was hired, the town said it would pay its share of his salary but would not let him anywhere near its schools.

Just before the Reverend Donnocker was to depart Boston for his new duties on the Cape, police in that city arrested him on a warrant from Maine. The charge was rape.

During his tenure in Maine, the Reverend Donnocker had left his wife and family in Brockton and moved in as a boarder with a family that belonged to his new congregation. The eldest daughter in this family had claimed that the reverend had forced himself on her, resulting in the arrest warrant. The Reverend Donnocker was hauled to Maine and held on $4,000 cash bail. The Sandwich School Committee had itself the biggest "I told you so" in Cape Cod history.

Sandwich's exuberance did nothing to quell Bourne's insistence that Donnocker was their man. "Innocent until proven guilty" was Bourne's position. When Sandwich called for a meeting to discuss the dismissal of the Reverend Donnocker, the Bourne School Committee refused to show, even though the meeting was held in their town. Bourne's holdout did not prevent Sandwich and Mashpee from voting to suspend the minister and begin a search for a new superintendent.

When the Reverend Donnocker went to trial in early October, the charge against him had been reduced to adultery. The alleged victim testified that the Reverend Donnocker had attacked her when the two were home alone in 1892; the Reverend Donnocker vehemently denied her charges, claiming that he had been studying in his room.

The jury sided with the victim and found the reverend guilty. At a joint school committee meeting a few weeks later, Sandwich and Mashpee called for another vote to officially oust Donnocker. This time the Bourne contingent showed up, but remained as contrary as ever, voting unanimously to allow the Reverend Donnocker retain his job. Bourne's support was not enough to outweigh the Sandwich and Mashpee coalition, who voted to award the superintendent job to H. S. Freeman.

Incredibly, Bourne refused to pay Freeman its share of the superintendent's salary during the eight months he ran Upper Cape schools. The town claimed it did not have the authority to fire Donnocker. Freeman sued, and the case eventually went all the way to the state supreme court, which in 1898 ordered Bourne to pay. The judges ruled that the school committee has the authority to dismiss a person if it "has reasonable cause to believe him to be an unfit person to hold a position." Apparently a conviction for adultery was cause enough.

Cape Cod
Confidence Games

There is a fine line between legitimate businessman and con artist, and the sandy earth of Cape Cod has always made it easy for some to smudge that line with a sweep of the toe. Some of the greatest and not-so-greatest swindlers in history have come from Cape Cod. In turn, confidence men have found a home on the Cape, revealing that residents can be as gullible as anyone.

We begin with the greatest swindle put over on the American people by a sitting president until Watergate. And it all happened on Cape Cod.

Hail to the Chief

A generation before any Kennedy ever gave thought to coming to Cape Cod, it was the summer home of our twenty-fourth president, Stephen Grover Cleveland. He was between presidential jobs from 1889 to 1893 when he purchased a cottage he called "Gray Gables." The large, rambling building sat at the mouth of Bourne's Monument River as it emptied into Buzzards Bay.

It's hard to gauge what Cape Codders thought of their new neighbor. During his first summer on the Cape, the town of Sandwich threw a reception for him. Sandwich, though, was more than five miles away from Gray Gables, and one wonders why the town of Bourne did not throw a party of its own. Could it have been that the bluenosed Cape Codders were offended by their new neighbor? Or was it the presidential election of 1884, one of the dirtiest political fights in history?

That election pitted Cleveland, the former governor of New York, against Senator James Blaine of Maine. When

President Grover Cleveland

Cleveland won the Democratic nomination in July, he looked to be an easy victor. Between the Democratic and Republican conventions, the world learned that Senator Blaine had been accepting perquisites from railroad interests in exchange for favorable legislation. To compensate, Blaine's fellow Republicans went in search of mud they could fling back.

Cleveland appeared outwardly to be the wrong kind of guy to attack. He was arrogant, short-tempered, and rude; but above all, he was honest. As mayor of Buffalo and later governor of New York, he had the reputation of being above reproach. To the Democratic Party, he must have appeared the perfect candidate to face the tainted Blaine. Perfect, that is, until the *Boston Journal* printed a front-page story that accused candidate Cleveland of having fathered a child out of wedlock.

Cape Cod Confidential

When his aides asked him what they should do about the scurrilous attack, Cleveland uttered what was to be one of his most famous lines: "Tell the truth." And the truth was, well, he had fathered a child out of wedlock.

In these days before exit polling, it is unknown how much effect the report of Cleveland's bastard had on the presidential race. As Election Day drew near, Democrats could be heard chanting in the streets, "Blaine, Blaine, James G. Blaine, continental liar from the state of Maine!" Republicans, in turn, would chant back, "Ma, Ma, where's my pa? He's in the White House, ha-ha-ha!" The Lincoln-Douglas debates, it was not.

Cleveland narrowly won election that year, but not on Cape Cod, where Blaine outpolled him by more than three to one. In Bourne, which of course did not know Mr. Cleveland would soon be a part-time resident, the vote was almost four to one for Blaine, 188 to 50.

Four years later, Cleveland ran for reelection against Benjamin Harrison. Even though President Cleveland received more votes than his opponent, the vagaries of the electoral college gave the election to Harrison. Cleveland retired from the presidency and began to take his summers on Cape Cod. In 1892 he ran again against Harrison. He received roughly the same number of votes as he had received in 1888, but this time he won them in the right places (namely New York), and he handily won election in both the popular vote and in the electoral college. Cape Cod had its first Summer White House.

Cleveland began 1893 as president for the second time. Little did he know that he would face the greatest professional and private challenges of his lifetime; in the middle of it all would be his precious summer home, Gray Gables.

It began on June 27, 1893, when the stock market crashed, heralding one of the worst economic downturns ever seen in the United States. Three days later, barely five months into his term, Grover Cleveland called for an emergency session of Congress to repeal the Sherman Silver Act, which he believed to be the cause of the country's economic troubles. Then he promptly vanished.

For the first time in the history of the United States, a sitting president disappeared so completely that the top elected officers in the country knew nothing of his whereabouts. The vice president did not know where the president had gone; nor did the Speaker of the House, or even the heads of his own Democratic Party. The United States was in a panic, and the president was nowhere to be found.

He reappeared six days later on Cape Cod. The *Oneida*, a yacht belonging to Elias C. Benedict, Cleveland's good friend from New York, quietly moored along the western shore of Cape Cod in Buzzards Bay. Grover Cleveland stepped off a launch and limped from the shore to Gray Gables. His aides announced that the president had had two ulcerated teeth removed during the voyage and that rheumatism in his foot and leg was acting up.

But rheumatism was not what ailed President Cleveland. Two of his teeth had been removed, that was true; but so had the entire left half of his upper jaw, cut away so that surgeons could get to the roof of his mouth where a malignant tumor was growing.

Cleveland was a man of passions: his love of fishing brought him to Cape Cod; his love of food had made him the fattest president, a record he held until William Howard Taft came to power. He also loved tobacco, and one of his most unappetizing habits was chewing cigars. In May, the president had noticed a rough spot the size of a quarter on the roof of his mouth. He delayed mentioning it to his doctor until June 18. White House physician Robert O'Reilly sent a sample of tissue to Johns Hopkins University, which confirmed the doctor's suspicion—it was cancer.

Dr. O'Reilly called in Cleveland's friend, New York surgeon Joseph Bryant. "Were it in my mouth, I would have it removed at once," Bryant told the president.

Cape Cod Confidential

The operation was conducted onboard the yacht *Oneida* July 1 as it steamed up the East River. Surgeons knocked out Cleveland with ether. To get to the roof of his mouth, the president sat in a chair, propped against the main mast in the yacht's saloon. A recent innovation in surgery from France, a special retractor, pulled back the president's bulbous left cheek. This ingenious device would mean that there would be no way to tell the president had had surgery—there would be no incision outside the mouth. A dentist removed his two left upper bicuspid teeth and Dr. Bryant took over with the electric knife. Once the rough area at the roof of the mouth was exposed, the team discovered the cancer had spread to Cleveland's left upper jaw, requiring its removal. Dr. Bryant then scraped out the soft, gray, gelatinous mass of cancerous tissue between the upper palate and the eye socket. He packed the cavity with gauze and ordered the president to bed. The operation took only thirty-one minutes.

Two days later, Cleveland was able to walk about the *Oneida*. On July 5, the yacht moored in Buzzards Bay at Gray Gables and let off its esteemed passenger with his severe case of "rheumatism."

The president's aides did everything they could to keep the ravenous press, curiosity seekers, even Vice President Adlai Stevenson, at bay. The remoteness of Gray Gables helped considerably.

President Cleveland's first appearance outside his summer home was within a few days after his arrival. "The President made his first fishing trip Monday (July 10) since he arrived at Gray Gables," reported the *Yarmouth Register*, Cape Cod's Republican newspaper. In an editorial, editor Charles Swift wrote, "It looks as if the President must sympathize with the boy who wanted a first-rate rainstorm; just rain enough to keep him from school, and not enough to prevent going a-fishing. His ailments are such that he can't see office seekers, but he manages to drop a line into Buzzards Bay occasionally."

According to the *Register*, "The party only went down the bay five miles and cast anchor off Wing's Neck. The President enjoyed the trip very much. This was the first day he has been seen since his arrival and he is looking unusually well."

Actually, the president looked awful, according to witnesses at the time. One reason he may have ventured outside Gray Gables was a story in the *New York Times* the day before. "The President Is All Right," read the headline. "Alarming Stories of His Illness Without Foundation."

> *BUZZARDS BAY, Mass, July 8—The assertion that President Cleveland is seriously afflicted with any malady is all nonsense. It is purely and simply "an invention of the enemy." The most favorable stories have been sent from here regarding his condition are the true stories. ... Dr. Bryant, who is giving Mr. Cleveland such slight medical attendance as may add to his comfort, says that he had only an ordinary, every-day toothache, and the ordinary application of cold steel had the ordinary results. Undoubtedly there is a vacancy along his jaw where a tooth once grew—but surely nothing more will be heard of its "cancerous growth."*

The *Register* reported the next week that "the President left Buzzards Bay on Monday (July 17) in steam yacht *Oneida* on a fishing excursion of two or three days." In truth, the only one doing any fishing on that trip was Dr. Bryant, who once again attacked Cleveland's mouth for what was believed to be the last vestiges of the cancer. After the president returned, the *Register* wrote, "President Cleveland says his rheumatism has left him and he feels perfectly well. But he has not yet extended an invitation to office seekers to pay him a friendly call."

How Cleveland was able to say anything defies explanation. His mouth was packed with cotton, and half his upper jaw was gone. Cleveland was never known for his elocution, but now he had become completely unintelligible. In less than three weeks he would be required to give a speech before Congress.

The solution was provided by a New York dentist, Kasson C. Gibson. Dr. Gibson came to Gray Gables and, after setting up a jury-rigged dental lab, managed to fashion an artificial jaw out of vulcanized rubber. It was a prosthesis Cleveland would wear for the rest of his life; no one but his closest friends and associates would ever know it was there.

On August 5, the president returned to Washington, and two days later he gave his address to Congress. He lasted, in total, four days in the Washington heat before he returned to Gray Gables to continue his recuperation. The story of his operation and the seriousness of his illness did not get out until September.

On September 9, the *Yarmouth Register* wrote, "The disquieting reports relating to the President's health that were rife when he first came to Buzzards Bay in July have been repeated quite circumstantially recently by Dr. Hasbrouck, an eminent New York dentist, who administered nitrous oxide gas and extracted two of the President's teeth, preparatory to the removal by Dr. Bryant of diseased portions of the bone of the upper jaw and the adjoining bone of the nose. ... What the ultimate result will be is a matter of uncertainty. Whether the development is of a cancerous nature is not disclosed; in fact, Dr. Hasbrouck did not know, because the microscopian examination was conducted by Dr. Bryant, but he had known similar cases in which the subjects had entirely recovered. This disclosure, which has every evidence of authenticity, explains Mr. Cleveland's seclusion at Buzzards Bay, his sudden return from Washington, and the constant presence since of Dr. Bryant with the President at Gray Gables."

By September, it did not matter who knew. By that time the president appeared before the Pan-American Medical Conference in Washington, looking fit and fully recovered from surgery. Although the Silverites put up a good fight, both houses of Congress overturned the Sherman Silver Act by October. America survived the panic, and Cleveland survived to finish his presidency.

You Can Run,
but You Can't Hide

While many look at Cape Cod as a place to escape the pressures of civilization, there are probably just as many who view Cape Cod as a place from which to escape.

Fleeing the Cape in the previous century was harder than in most places, particularly if you were running to avoid your responsibilities. Cape Codders were a well-traveled bunch, roaming the seven seas in their great ships. Odds were pretty good that no matter where you went in the world, you were likely to run into someone you knew.

Some folks were just plain stupid about this fact. The best places to go to avoid Cape Codders were inland. But a lot of attempted runaways could not keep from living on or near the coast.

Take the case of Stephen Sherman. In 1889, Sherman lived in Yarmouth where he worked at the town almshouse, a facility that attended to the poor. In February he disappeared, leaving behind wife and children. Last seen at the train station, he apparently was heading for New York. Also boarding that same train was a young, attractive woman—a stranger to the people of Yarmouth. She, too, purchased a ticket to New York.

Sherman had told his wife that he would be returning by a certain date. When that date came and went, the townspeople and Mrs. Sherman put two and two together. Her husband had absconded with another woman.

Slightly more than three months later, a man and woman who called themselves "Mr. and Mrs. Daniel Brown" got off the stage in Kittery, Maine. Kittery at that time was a tiny community, across the Piscataqua River from Portsmouth, New Hampshire Fugitives fleeing persecution from the Massachusetts Bay Colony had settled it in the 1600s. As a result, the townspeople were genetically predisposed to paranoia and not very amenable when it came to strangers.

The Browns seemed to go out of their way not to melt into the background. For one, each clearly was wearing at least three layers of clothes. The denizens of Kittery speculated the Browns did this so that they could make a quick change and disguise themselves if spotted by their pursuers. A more rational explanation is that this cut down on the number of bags they had to carry, which would make it easier for them to make a quick exit, if caught.

The second clue that this couple was up to no good came from their own lips. They requested the driver hired at the station to take them to a boardinghouse where they would be "unmolested and undisturbed by inquisitive people."

What clinched everyone's suspicions was the Browns' claim that they had arrived in Maine "all the way from Oklahoma." Had they said, "New York" or "Connecticut," they might have been left alone. But no one in his right mind would travel all the way to Maine from Oklahoma. This was particularly odd considering that only a few days before, the territory had been opened up to homesteaders.

Cape Cod Confidential

The townspeople began to watch the Browns' every move. Not only did they spy on what the couple did, but they paid special attention to what they didn't do. That they *did not* receive mail was keenly noted and increased the certainty that the Browns were on the lam.

The Browns began to notice the extra attention, and in an effort to relieve themselves of all prying eyes, made their final and biggest mistake. They moved to one of the islands in the Isle of Shoals, on property owned by a wealthy Boston man.

One day, Mr. Brown was walking along the shore when he encountered a fisherman who appeared to recognize him. The fisherman asked Brown where he had come from and Brown answered, "South Yarmouth." He must have meant "South Yarmouth, Oklahoma," but the fisherman, who frequently harbored in Barnstable, took him to mean "South Yarmouth, Massachusetts."

Mr. Brown later amended his statement by claiming to have come from Centerville, but it was too late. When the fisherman made his way back to the Cape, he mentioned to some locals his encounter with Mr. Brown. The jig was up.

Leaving the Cape
to Forge a New Career

Professor R. E. Wilson arrived in Gainesville, Texas, in the early 1890s. His manners and speech were clearly those of an easterner. He came to Texas not to seek his fortune (for he was already wealthy), but to build a new life.

Opportunity soon knocked. The job of principal at Gainesville High School opened, and the school board offered Professor Wilson the job. He quickly built the small institute into a successful secondary school.

The Gay '90s were not gay for everyone. The period was marked by the worst economic depression in U.S. history. Men and women fled rural areas such as Gainesville for the big city, where jobs could be found. However, one couldn't get a job if one had no skills. Thus was born the "business college."

A group of investors approached Professor Wilson with the hope he would agree to start such a business college in Gainesville. Wilson agreed and resigned from Gainesville High School.

"Gainesville College" opened in what had been the mansion of cattle baron Zack Addington. During his four years as a principal, Professor Wilson had developed excellent contacts among the state's education leaders. He soon recruited a top-notch group of administrators and teachers.

Professor Wilson was so highly respected in Gainesville that no one found it suspicious when he began taking out a series of loans at several of the town's banks. For collateral, he presented notes signed by Gainesville's leading citizens.

In January 1899, Professor Wilson mysteriously disappeared. Gainesville's citizens were shocked to learn that there was a warrant out for his arrest. The professor had been charged with forgery. The notes that Wilson had used to obtain his loans had all been forgeries. When a proper accounting had been made, authorities estimated he had made off with somewhere between $20,000 and $30,000.

Police got their first clue as to Wilson's whereabouts a few months later, when the professor sent a letter to a friend in Gainesville. The letter carried the postmark of Kendall Green, Kansas, and its contents revealed that Wilson had relatives somewhere near Boston. Texas authorities contacted the state detectives in Massachusetts, who began distributing pictures of Professor Wilson. Although they did not discover his whereabouts, they did learn exactly who he was.

"Professor Wilson" was, in fact, a Sandwich man named Charles W. Robinson. Robinson had come from one of the best families in town, with roots extending back to the early settlers of the Plymouth colony. He had left the Cape as a young man and moved to Brockton, where he was able to win appointment as clerk of the municipal court. Throughout the 1880s, Robinson ran in the best circles in Brockton, which at the time was an economic powerhouse in Massachusetts. He bought a beautiful home on Warren Avenue and became friends with many of the leading businessmen and elected officials.

In addition to his clerking duties, Robinson also ran an office of the New York Stock Exchange. Although he had no children, his keen interest in education led to his election to several terms on the Brockton School Committee.

Then, on October 26, 1890, Robinson vanished. And with him disappeared an astonishing $100,000, the result of forged collateral notes as well as phony stock investments. Until Charles Ponzi came along some thirty years later, it would be one of the largest frauds in Massachusetts history.

Everyone had thought Robinson had fled to South America. Instead he had gone to Texas. When he left Texas, everyone was sure he had gone to Mexico. Instead, as authorities were to learn later, he had come home.

He would not turn up again for another four years. In 1903, Robinson paid a visit to a former friend in Brockton. He confessed that he had been living in Warwick, Rhode Island, where, going by the name of Charles Wilson, he had become the principal of a village grammar school. He was assistant superintendent of the local Baptist society. He ran the local improvement society. He had been reappointed only the week before to the principalship, but he had not shown up for work.

Robinson told his friend that he was on his way to Sandwich to visit his parents before "leaving the country for good." By the time police got word of his whereabouts, his trail had once again gone cold.

Before leaving, he sent the *Brockton Enterprise* newspaper a ninety-nine-page apologia. He wanted to "square accounts." His life on the lam had not been an easy one, he explained. Yet wherever he went, he tried to make things better, be it in the church or in the schools.

"Probably he has paid a hundred times the amount he has received in anguish of the bitterest kind," noted one newspaper editor. "But still the bill is unsettled."

There's a Fair
(and a Scam) in the Air

Today's county fairs are not as much fun as they used to be. In the old days, the midway was a playground for fleece artists, where a huckster could strip the local rube of his last nickel with a line of bull, a baseball, and three carefully weighted milk bottles.

The life of a carney has never been easy. In bygone times, it was downright dangerous. The shooting gallery, once a staple, enabled amateur marksmen to try their luck with real guns. In 1946, a carney by the name of Clarence Rees took a bullet in the gut during a carnival run in Orleans. A five-year-old boy had reached up and pulled the trigger of one of the .22 rifles that was lying on the counter just as Rees was changing a target.

Rees survived the shooting. Police did not charge the little boy with assault with a dangerous weapon, but he probably didn't win a stuffed animal either.

Another staple of carnivals, long departed, was the girlie show. In 1941, Provincetown police raided a carnival after sending in one of its men undercover. "I paid 20 cents to enter the place," Patrolman Robert Cairns said later. "After the first performance was over, (the manager of the show) said we could see more if we paid another 20 cents, and that the show was for men only." Cairns bought a ticket and was led to the other side of the stage where two woman danced using "hula movements" and took off their clothes. The emcee and the women were arrested at the "climax of their performance," according to a *Cape Cod Standard Times* report.

All were found guilty a few days later of "presenting an immoral show." The defense lawyer attempted to argue that the show was not obscene because no minors had been present. "Do you mean to tell me that the type of performance described in court today would not be indecent if presented before a group of 100-year-old men who had been married five times each?" the judge asked.

The defense lawyer said no. "It would not be indecent unless young people were present." When that didn't work, the lawyer pointed out that the show had played elsewhere on the Cape without complaint.

Neither argument swayed the judge. The two women were sentenced to a year's probation. The show manager and another man were each fined $50.

Not all stories involve carneys and other promoters coming here. Cape Codders are more than up to the challenge of scamming the unwary. In 1892, newspapers all over the country were writing about the upcoming World's Fair in Chicago. The pavilions for this fair, in honor of the 400th anniversary of the landing of Columbus, would be the most elaborate and spectacular ever seen. But few things generated as much interest as Provincetown's proposed pavilion, which would feature a real, live sperm whale. An old whaling captain, Amos Chapman, promised to capture the beast and see it brought alive to the Midwest.

Newspapers wrote extensively about the latest attraction. No one, it seemed, bothered to check the story. If they had, they would have found that Capt. Amos Chapman, while a real person, was no whaling captain. He had gone on a whaling voyage once in his youth, but had abandoned the sea for a lucrative business selling fish and meat on Charles Street in Boston. At 300 pounds, it was doubtful whether Chapman could have lifted himself out of his chair, much less taken to the sea to capture a sperm whale.

Who fell hardest for the joke? According to the newspaperman who spread the hoax, the ones most fooled were the old whalers in New Bedford who "took the thing in dead earnest and never once hinted the thing was not feasible."

Escaping by the Skin of Our Tithe

There's a bumper-sticker slogan that surely must have been written by a Yankee Cape Codder: "In God we trust—all others pay cash." Sometimes, though, you can't even trust God, or at least those who claim to be God's messenger.

The Reverend George Dunbar came to Cape Cod in the early 1890s to serve the Methodists of South Yarmouth. As one source described him, he was "an earnest, energetic and emotional young preacher." He was a rising star in the world of Methodism, a fiery presence who enraptured the faithful throughout southern New England with his compelling preaching. He became a popular figure at camp meetings, his dynamic presence impressing anyone who happened to fall within the reach of his voice. Everyone who came in contact with the Reverend Dunbar just knew the Lord had big plans for him.

He began his walk with God in a small Methodist church in South Yarmouth. Within a few months, a larger and wealthier congregation that hailed from Eastham and Orleans lured him away.

Bigger churches mean bigger headaches for ministers, usually in the form of church politics. Almost from the outset, the Reverend Dunbar began to butt heads with the unofficial patriarch of the Orleans Methodist church, Captain Mayo.

It began early on in his ministry, when the Reverend Dunbar complained that his parsonage was too small. He asked the church trustees for $400 to pay for an expansion of the meager home. The trustees, led by Captain Mayo, thought the sum was too large for their congregation and denied the minister's petition. This proved no obstacle for the ambitious Reverend Dunbar, who offered to go out to the congregation and obtain the subscriptions necessary to cover the cost of the construction.

In no time at all, the preacher returned with pledges that would more than pay for the project, and the board of trustees reluctantly gave its blessing. The Reverend Dunbar, however, had made an enemy of Captain Mayo, a man who was accustomed to getting his way in church matters. More and more, however, the trustees and the rest of the congregation began to side with the Reverend Dunbar, and more and more, Captain Mayo and his supporters found their influence eroding.

The schism only widened once construction on the improvements to the parsonage were underway. To Captain Mayo and his friends, the reverend was not making a few necessary improvements but building "a palatial residence." One of Captain Mayo's crowd even quit the board of trustees over the perceived opulence of the minister's quarters.

Later, an accounting showed the minister had actually spent $900 for the renovations, $500 more than the original budget. Suddenly there arose whispers around the village of borrowed sums and unpaid debts. The Reverend Dunbar's supporters attributed the source of the gossip to Captain Mayo's friends and associates. Several individuals came forward to say that the Reverend Dunbar owed them money, but that they did not have the slightest fear that they would not be paid.

In 1893, the Reverend Dunbar announced he was moving to Stoughton to assume the pulpit there. Just as suddenly, many of those who had expressed confidence in the integrity of the minister's creditors began to call on him to find out exactly when they were going to be paid.

A. T. Newcomb, owner of the local hardware store, dropped in on the Reverend Dunbar to inquire about a $48 bill. The minister met the man at the door, invited him in, and the two had a pleasant chat. Newcomb was halfway home before he realized he had forgotten to ask about the debt.

Another merchant made an appointment to meet with the young minister to discuss his obligation. When the minister failed to show, the merchant ignored that part of the Lord's Prayer concerning "debts" and reported the overdue obligation to the sheriff. That action suddenly prompted everyone in Orleans and Eastham to compare notes. When they did, they discovered that the Reverend Dunbar owed more than just thirty pieces of silver.

The minister by this time had left for Stoughton. The trail of bad paper he had left behind created a scandal that set tongues wagging for miles.

There were still those who supported the Reverend Dunbar, despite the mounting evidence of his swindling. Captain Mayo's wife happened to be writing to the captain's sister, Sarah Mayo, about the minister's misdeeds. "I hope you have not been foolish enough to lend him any money," Mrs. Mayo wrote the sister, who coincidentally enough happened to live in Stoughton not far from the Reverend Dunbar.

Sarah Mayo had just moved to Stoughton from Orleans, where she had been one of the minister's biggest supporters. So much a supporter that she and the woman she shared a house with had loaned the Reverend Dunbar exactly $2,197.59.

When Captain Mayo learned that his own sister had been fleeced, he took the matter to the regional Methodist church council in Providence. The elders in the church stripped the Reverend Dunbar of his raiment. His brothers came forward to pay his debts.

Captain Mayo finally had his revenge. His sister did not share in his glee. One day a friend asked her about the miserable state of her finances. Rather than seek sympathy, Sarah Mayo simply replied, "It's gone for a good cause," and left it at that.

Law & Order

Law & Order

Justice, as Daniel Webster once said, "is the
ligament which holds civilized beings and
civilized nations together." The judicial
system on Cape Cod, as Webster learned
during his time here, was strange in its own
right. Once while trying a case in Barnstable,
Webster's lawyer colleague on the other side
of the case needed to enter into evidence
a description of one of the harbors in the
Hawaiian Islands. There was no need,
Webster soon found out, because seven of the
twelve jurors had been there many times.

The following sketches cover the gamut of
Cape Cod and the legal system, from judges
and lawyers to jailers and prisoners, proving,
as Webster put it while writing to Cape
Codders, "Gentlemen, the nature of your
population is somewhat peculiar."

The Cape Cod
Mining Company

Man's crimes are his worst enemies, following him like
shadows, till they drive his steps into the pit he dug.
                              —Creon, a dead Greek writer

Confession, it is said, is good for the soul. For at least one convict in the state prison in 1849, the benefits of unloading his conscience proved to be the cure to all his ills.

On a spring day more than 150 years ago, William Phelps asked to see Warden Robinson of the prison in Charlestown. Serving time for robbing the state arsenal in Boston and a jewelry shop in Lynn, Phelps had more than eight years remaining on his sentence. In the minds of state correctional authorities, Phelps was strictly a small-time hood.

What Phelps revealed to the warden shattered that image. Phelps confessed that he had been the mastermind behind a bank heist in what is today Wheeling, West Virginia, that netted more than $50,000 in gold. Furthermore, he had buried the loot on Cape Cod, near the village of Osterville.

Prisons in the nineteenth century were, as they are today, filled with men who claimed to be innocent. It was rare that a convict confessed to a crime for which he was not even a suspect. Still, Warden Robinson wanted to verify Phelps's story. He sent for the president of the Wheeling bank, who agreed to meet with the prisoner.

Although there is no record of what Phelps told the banker, whatever he said convinced Warden Robinson that the convict was telling the truth. The chief official of the Massachusetts penal system decided that day to embark on an expedition to Cape Cod to recover the treasure.

Phelps told Robinson that he would have to show the warden the exact hiding place. The prisoner, the warden, and a Charlestown city marshal named Nichols left the prison armed with picks and shovels for a little gold digging on Cape Cod.

The warden had told no one of his plans. The three "miners" managed to arrive in the Cape Cod woods without attracting any attention.

Phelps showed the warden and the marshal where he had buried the loot. The party commenced digging, but did so cautiously. One man dug, while the other stood guard over Phelps. In the spirit of cooperation, Phelps himself even took a turn behind the pick and shovel.

Phelps had buried the bank gold deep. It took most of a day, but the men managed to excavate a giant hole, one so large that the man digging could not get out without the help of one of the others. Phelps announced that he was certain they were about to strike his cache. Marshal Nichols clawed at the earth with his pick, and Warden Robinson stood on the lip of the hole, watching intently, expecting any second to hear the pick strike the golden coins.

The warden was so consumed by gold fever that he lost track of Phelps. The prisoner had slid directly behind

Robinson and, as the warden leaned over the hole, Phelps gave him a little shove.

According to at least one account, Phelps stood over the two men, laughed at their foolishness and then threw a few shovelfuls of dirt on top of them for spite. Phelps later denied this. The warden and marshal were armed, so he did what anyone else in his position would do—he ran.

One can picture the warden and the marshal trying to climb out of the pit, only to find no purchase thanks to the sandy soil of Cape Cod. Phelps must have gotten a pretty good head start, for by the time the men managed to clamber out and reach local authorities, he was long gone.

Warden Robinson had a tremendous amount of explaining to do. The Boston newspapers had a field day with the escape, thanks not only to the warden's stupidity, but also to his unfortunate timing. The California Gold Rush was the big news of the year, and the tale of Warden Robinson and the "Charlestown and Cape Cod Mining Company" gave the story legs that kept it alive for weeks.

Even the Wheeling bank president, although several hundred miles away, found he could not escape the story. Eventually he had to issue a denial that Phelps had duped him. "I was convinced that Phelps' story of having a large sum of money was a falsehood," he told the newspapers weeks after the story of the escape had become public. "I sent to the cashier of our bank the following message: 'Arrived this morning—leaving this evening—all humbug.'"

Just as the story died down, it blazed back to life when authorities apprehended Phelps in his old haunts in Boston.

According to Phelps, after he had tipped the warden, he ran for "six miles" through the woods. He then wandered for four days and nights, eventually finding shelter with an Indian family, one presumes in nearby Mashpee. From there he managed to catch a ride on a small boat that took him to Boston.

He hid briefly in Maine, but then returned to Boston, where he was captured three months after his escape.

The newspapers dubbed Phelps "the Cape Cod Miner." Many people thought he should be released. "Out of respect for the skill in which he effected his escape there was a strong feeling of regret manifested yesterday when his recapture became known," wrote the *Boston Post*. A petition containing more than 200 signatures demanded Phelps' freedom.

The Cape Cod Miner, however, served the remainder of his sentence. Although he entered prison as a petty criminal, he left it as a folk hero, knowing that for generations his exploits would be remembered on Cape Cod.

Dying for a New Prison
on Cape Cod

Dying for a New Prison
on Cape Cod

If these stories have shown anything, it's that the old maxim—"Those who ignore history are doomed to repeat it"—is only half true. The fact is we are all doomed to repeat history, regardless of whether we remember it or not. A better way of putting it has been wonderfully condensed onto the bumper sticker which reads (as edited), "Same stuff, different day."

A perfect example is the Barnstable County Jail and House of Correction, overcrowded. The county is building a new one, because the old one has been filled to far beyond its capacity.

During the Civil War, Barnstable County was in the exact same position. The old jail could not safely contain another prisoner. Before the war began, the county had operated two jails, one in Barnstable and one in Provincetown, but that became too expensive, and the facility at the Cape tip was closed. The sheriff begged for a new jail, or at least an addition, but the county commissioners would not budge.

In April 1863, the jail had enough room for four new prisoners. As luck would have it, the Barnstable Superior Court session looked to have exactly four cases before it where the defendants would be subject to jail time if convicted.

The grand jury on April 6 returned four indictments. The panel charged Ziba Ellis and Asa Mathews for stealing cable and other materials from the schooner *Magnet*, which had been tied up in Hyannis Harbor. As they had been caught red-handed, the two pleaded guilty and were fined $500. Being thieves, they did not have that kind of money, so they were sent to the Barnstable House of Correction instead.

The next case was a minor one. E. C. White had allowed kids to play billiards at his establishment. Fined $10, which fortunately he happened to have with him, he was allowed to leave.

Next up were Fontenella Cowett and Gustavus Pells, who were charged with breaking and entering. The court had no choice but to continue their case and release them on their own recognizance. What had set them free had been the murder of poor Isaiah Wright of Sandwich.

That previous winter, Wright had been returning home from his brother's house when someone met him and shot him dead. Suspicion fell on the Holways, the family of Wright's wife. Only a few days before the superior court session, the sheriff had arrested Wright's father-in-law, John Holway, and Holway's son James for murder.

Judge Ezra Wilkinson could have freed the Holways, whose case would not come before the grand jury for months, instead of Cowett and Pells, but apparently in the judicial world, those suspected of murder are considered more of a danger to society than those charged with breaking and entering. The Holways stayed and Cowett and Pells were free to go, "the county being too poor to continue that class of offenders," wrote the *Yarmouth Register*.

Two weeks later, the Holways came before a judge. The district attorney charged that either the Holways had committed the murder or they knew who had. The family had all been part of a conspiracy to kill Isaiah Wright, a conspiracy that included Wright's wife.

Only the Holways had motive to kill Wright, the district attorney said.

The ill feelings toward Wright had begun back when the victim had proposed marriage to a Holway. While the couple was in love, Wright came to disdain her family and eventually broke off the engagement. The family threatened to sue for breach of promise, so Wright relented. After the nuptials, there had been nothing but trouble.

On the night of the murder, Mrs. Wright implored her husband to take soup to his brother, something he had never done, nor had his wife ever suggested. During Wright's visit, his father-in-law mysteriously showed up for an unexpected visit. When Wright got up to leave, the elder Holway also got up and stood by the window, which the district attorney claimed was a signal. Holway remained with Wright's brother, and within a minute of the young man's departure the sound of a rifle or pistol shot could be heard. Wright's brother went out to find Isaiah lying face down in the path, dying. He was too far gone to say who had killed him.

Wright was soon joined by John Holway and, in another remarkable coincidence, by Wright's wife. Just before Holway and his daughter entered the home of Wright's brother, the two exchanged whispers, which the district attorney claimed was further evidence of their conspiracy.

Based on the testimony of the hearing, the judge ordered the Holways held until the next sitting of the grand jury in September. That same week, the state House of Representatives passed a bill that ordered the county commissioners to tax the citizens of Barnstable County $13,000 for a new jail. By that June, the bill had passed the Senate.

And what of the Holways? That September their case came before the grand jury, which decided there was not enough evidence to warrant a murder charge. Isaiah Wright's murder remains unsolved to this day.

Eleven Angry Men and the Cape Codder

In the annals of crime on the high seas, no more lurid tale exists than of the murder aboard the sailing ship *Herbert Fuller*. She had set sail from Boston on July 2, 1896, headed for South America with a load of timber. At the helm was Capt. Charles Nash, accompanied by his wife, Laura. The crew consisted of first mate Thomas Bram and second mate August Blomberg. There was also a steward and six crewmen, and a passenger, Lester Monks, who was traveling "for his health."

The captain, his wife, Bram, Blomberg, and Monks had quarters in the after-cabin. The crew and steward slept up front. In the early morning hours of July 14, Bram was officer of the deck. Two of the seamen were on lookout and a crewman named Charles Brown was at the wheel.

Shortly before two o'clock, a scream woke Monk. He listened, and over the normal creaking and groaning of a ship thought he could make out a "gurgling" noise. He arose and

116

entered the captain's cabin, finding the cot overturned, and the captain dead on the floor. Monk went into Mrs. Nash's room and could not tell if she was in bed, although he could make out the bedclothes stained by something dark.

Monk went above deck, found Bram, and told him of the discovery. Both men went below and confirmed that both the Captain and Mrs. Nash were dead, their heads opened like broken eggs.

The next morning, Bram advised the crew of the murder. When second mate Blomberg did not come up, Bram entered his cabin and found him lying on his back, his feet crossed, and his head cut open to his brain.

The crew suspected Brown, and clapped him in irons. Brown then claimed he saw Bram in the captain's cabin the night of the murder, so the crew chained up Bram. On July 21, the *Herbert Fuller* sailed into Nova Scotia. Bram was interrogated by a detective from the United States who later testified:

> *When Mr. Bram came into my office, I said to him: "Bram, we are trying to unravel this horrible mystery." I said: "Your position is rather an awkward one. I have had Brown in this office, and he made a statement that he saw you do the murder." He said: "He could not have seen me. Where was he?" I said: "He states he was at the wheel." "Well," he said, "he could not see me from there."*

This was taken to be a confession, and Bram stood trial in federal court in Boston on charges of murder on the high seas. Fortunately, the jury included a man familiar with the ocean, Charles Howes of Chatham.

The trial in the winter of 1897 was long and tedious. As luck would have it, Howes was around to provide the comic relief. During the defense attorney's closing argument, in which he attempted to sway the jury with his oratory, Howes suddenly butted in from the jury box.

"You didn't state that sentence right," he interrupted.

"What is that?" Bram's attorney asked.

"You didn't state that sentence right," Howes repeated.

The judge ordered Howes to stand and explain himself.

"He says that Charles Brown said that he shot at a man," Howes said. "I contend that he said he was told he shot at a man."

"It will be better for you to keep your recollection of the evidence to yourself and not interrupt the argument," the judge chastised Howes. "The district attorney will call attention to it if it is not correct."

The district attorney agreed that he would speak up if the defense ever misspoke, and Howes kept his mouth shut—until the case went to the jury.

The first vote of the jury was eight to four in favor of conviction. After a full twenty-four hours of debate, it was eleven to one—with Howes the lone dissenting juror. The Cape Cod man flat out did not believe Brown could have seen Bram. Thanks to the persuasion of the eleven other jurors, Howes finally changed his vote to guilty. Bram was sentenced to death.

The U.S. Supreme Court overturned the case on the grounds that Bram's confession was really no confession at all. The government tried Bram again, and the new jury found him guilty again, sentencing him to life in prison.

In 1914, the mystery writer Mary Roberts Rinehart studied the Bram case and wrote a novelized treatment of it called "The After House." Rinehart fingered Charles Brown as the killer, the idea being he could have lashed the wheel, committed the murders and returned with no one being the wiser. Impressed, President Woodrow Wilson gave Bram a full pardon in 1919.

Charles Howes, if he were still alive, would have been tickled that justice had been done. However, back during the original trial in 1897, when the theory of Brown lashing the wheel for five minutes was presented, a bunch of old Cape Cod sea captains who had hundreds of years of experience on the water between them agreed that it was "incredible," that there was not a ship ever built that could have lasted thirty seconds with the wheel lashed and unmanned.

The Escape-Proof Jail?

George H. Cash, the man in charge of the Barnstable County Jail and House of Correction, had a perfect attendance record. In the three years he had been running the jail, no prisoner had so much as even tried to escape. According to the *Boston Evening Record* of 1897, there was good reason for this. Cash was not operating a jail; he was running a country club.

The *Evening Record* exposed the shocking conditions at the Barnstable jail on the front page of its February 6 edition. The newspaper detailed how a convicted embezzler, Emil Knappe, had been seen on the streets outside the jail in the company of the jailer's wife. Even more shocking, Knappe was teaching Mrs. Cash how to ride a bicycle. The newspaper also learned that Knappe assisted the Cash family with maintaining their personal accounts even though he was serving a five-year sentence for bilking the Springfield National Bank out of thousands of dollars.

Two weeks earlier, one of the prisoners, Lewis Rogers, had been seen driving cows from the jail to a pasture some distance away. Rogers, who was serving time as a member of a Harwich burglary ring, was unescorted. "The air was invigorating and the sun was bright and the distance is just about right for a pleasant walk," the *Evening Record* wrote.

The Boston newspaper managed to keep the story alive for weeks. There were more tawdry tales to tell. Joseph Variose, known around Barnstable as "Joe the Portagee," also drove the prison's cows. Joe had been convicted of adultery, and in this respect the county jail's power of rehabilitation proved a complete failure. The *Evening Record* discovered that while Variose was supposed to be tending the herd, he was instead nursing the affections of young lady named Rosa, who was employed as a maid at one of the local hotels.

Variose managed to win an early pardon from the county jail on the grounds that he was suffering from tuberculosis. "Rosa was quite as much overjoyed as her suitor," the *Evening Record* wrote. Before the couple could take up a life together, Variose needed to travel to Boston to restore his health. He borrowed $80 from Rosa, which was on top of the $30 he had borrowed from her earlier, supposedly to be used to win his early release.

Whatever treatment Variose found in Boston, it must have been magical, the *Evening Record* wrote. "Within a very brief period Joe celebrated his wedding festivities in New Bedford." His new bride's name, unfortunately, was not Rosa.

Rosa was pregnant, and when she informed her employers of her situation, they had Variose arrested. He awaited trial in the Barnstable jail, but this time his cow-herding privileges had been revoked.

The conditions at the Barnstable County Jail and House of Correction came as no surprise to the state commission on prisons. "Barnstable county jail has always been the same," Herbert Ward of Newton, a member of the commission, told an

Evening Record reporter. "Conditions there were just as easy for the prisoners before you were born as they are now. What else could one reasonably expect in such a small jail, where there are never over a handful of prisoners and where there is nothing to put the men to work on? They might just as well give bicycle lessons and drive the cows home as do anything else."

In March, members of the joint Legislative Committee on Prisons paid a surprise visit to the Barnstable jail. What did

Boston Evening Record

SATURDAY FEBRUARY 6 1897.

"IN JAIL" ON THE CAPE,

But Knappe Gave Bicycle Lessons to the Jailer's Wife.

SUMMER SPORTS AT THE FREE STATE HOTEL AT BARNSTABLE, SOME-TIMES STYLED A JAIL.

they find? "That the place was a prison in name only," said Representative Douglass of Boston. "Upon entering the prison our ears were greeted by the sound of a harmonica proceeding from the basement. We found three of the long-term men, one of whom had been sentenced for five years for forgery, at work pumping the water for the use of the prison and the surrounding buildings.

"In the kitchen of the jail another long-term man was found officiating in the capacity as cook," Representative Douglass continued. "It was ascertained that the remaining one of the five enjoyed the privileges attached to the position of cook to the keeper's family. Chairman Cook (Senator Marcus Cook) asked Keeper Cash if any restrictions were placed upon the long-term men. He replied that they had the run of the building, and in case of necessity were occasionally sent to the village upon different errands."

Both Cash and his wife were ordered to testify before the committee. When asked about the bicycle-riding incident, the couple confirmed the story. When asked if prisoners were acting as servants for the Cash household, the jailer replied that the county gave him a "pittance" of $350 per year to run the prison. On such a relatively small sum, he needed the prisoners' labor to run the county farm and perform other duties.

In the end, it was all much ado about nothing. Or at least, nothing that anyone was willing to do anything about. Both the state House and Senate took up the case of the Barnstable County Jail and House of Correction, but neither body seemed too excited about the prospect of conducting an investigation. The legislators from the Cape demanded an investigation, but said that the joint Legislative Committee on Prisons should not be the body to conduct it, as several members had demonstrated a lack of common sense. In the end, the entire affair faded away, and not even the *Boston Evening Record* could keep it alive. Jailer George Cash kept his job, and the county prisons remained in control of the county government.

Cape Cod Confidential

The *Boston Evening Record*, however, was not so fortunate; the newspaper lasted until 1929, when it merged with the Boston *American*. Today whatever is left of the *Record* survives with the Boston *Herald*.

Doing Time Moving
Planet Earth

Rather than cast prisoners into the pits of hell, more than one Massachusetts legislator in the nineteenth century thought the pits of the Cape Cod town of Bourne would be more appropriate. Not that there is really much difference.

In 1897, the state legislature was once again hearing proposals to dig a canal from Cape Cod Bay to Buzzards Bay through Bourne. The proposal had been kicking around since the Pilgrims, only this time the state prisons and county jails were at or beyond capacity. Before long, someone came up with the idea to kill two jailbirds with one stone.

In a hearing on March 5, Willard Howland came before the Legislative Committee on Harbors and Public Lands to propose a canal be dug using prisoners as laborers. He told the committee that convict labor had been used with great success on public-works projects in England. And in 1897, there was plenty of convict labor to be found.

"There are in the prisons of the commonwealth able to perform such work, about 5,000 men. Today they are employed to the extent of about 2,500 or about 48 percent, in a manufacturing enterprise yet the product of that labor brings a return to the commonwealth of about $138,000 per year," he said. It cost the state about $900,000 to feed and house the prisoners, which meant that the state was losing money on its captive labor force.

Building the canal with prison labor would be more lucrative, and Howland even hinted that the state could make money on the deal.

The initial reaction, at least by Cape newspapers, was to oppose the plan. Over the past fifteen years, there had been dozens of proposals to construct the canal, and only once had someone managed enough capital to actually start construction (only to run out of money and, from there, be run out of town). Cape Codders, especially those in Sandwich and Bourne, had become somewhat jaded over the years with various canal-construction proposals; most were believed frauds.

"The proposition to unload all the state convicts on Cape Cod does not suit our people," wrote one local newspaper. "That is rather a worse crowd than the ordinary canal operators."

The case for prisoners as ditch diggers drummed up more support the following year. In a report to the legislature, state prison Superintendent F. G. Pettigrove thought using prisoners to dig the canal was an excellent idea, although he was not in favor of using convicts in state prisons, but instead those in county jails. Some 2,000 men would be available, he wrote, and it would take an estimated 6 years and $2 million to build the canal.

Such a plan would ease prison overcrowding, according to a Warden Bridges of the state prison—not because the prisoners would be moved to the Cape, but because criminals would trip over themselves fleeing the state. A good number of those incarcerated in the state prison were there for vagrancy, he said. Tramps do not like to work, according to Warden Bridges, and they would leave Massachusetts rather than work.

Like countless other canal-digging proposals, Howland's scheme died without ever reaching the floor of the legislature. Someone else eventually built the canal without the aid of prisoners fifteen years later.

The idea of Cape Cod as penal colony, however, would not go away. It resurfaced forty years later. In 1937, the state of Georgia sought extradition of an escaped prisoner, James Cunningham, who had escaped from a chain gang and had been recaptured in Massachusetts. Governor Hurley of Massachusetts refused to send Cunningham back, calling the Georgia's chain-gang system "inhuman." A small disagreement, it appeared, and nothing more was heard about it until September. That was when Georgia Governor Rivers freed a convicted bookie, Fleming Willis, on the condition that he spend his parole in Massachusetts.

The peach really hit the pit when the Georgia governor suggested that Massachusetts establish a penal colony on Cape Cod. One newspaper pundit suggested that the idea came because the canal separated it from the mainland, making it a perfect Devil's Island. However, the real reason was that the Cape was home to the largest public-works project in the state, the construction of an army base to be known as Camp Edwards.

The same day, Governor Rivers paroled Fleming Willis, eight chain-gang convicts in Georgia overpowered a guard and escaped. Everyone presumed that they were headed for Cape Cod.

The Cape was in an uproar, but as quickly as it was proposed, the proposed Cape Cod Penal Colony faded from the headlines. Seven years later, in the final months of World War II, a German prisoner-of-war camp opened at Camp Edwards, over the objection of many Cape Codders.

The prisoners themselves silenced critics. In the fall of 1944, they harvested much of Cape Cod's cranberry crop, which had been languishing due to a war-incurred labor shortage. When a hurricane slammed into the Cape in September, crews of German POWs removed much of the fallen timber.

Cape Cod as Penal Colony probably didn't seem such a bad idea after all.

Pleading Guilty to a Murder No One Could Prove

W e've seen it on every cop TV show: a murder is committed, the police scour the city for a suspect, and into the station walks a disheveled man who confesses to the murder. The officers politely take the man's statement, all the while nodding and winking to each other. Eventually the man is hustled out, and someone makes a remark about cranks.

But how often does someone walk into the station and confess to a murder that no one can prove happened?

In the winter of 1881–1882, Frank Goodwin languished in the Worcester jail on charges of breaking and entering. He announced to his captors his desire to come clean about a murder three years before in Barnstable. In the fall of 1878, he said, he broke out of the Westboro Reform School and escaped to Barnstable, where he worked for a cranberry bog owner named Everett Childs. Goodwin said he remained on the Cape until he could be certain the passions of his pursuers had cooled, and then he traveled to Boston.

"I met two fellows—one of them from New York—who were out of a job and anxious to find work," Goodwin recalled three years later. "I told them we could get work on the cranberry bogs at Barnstable, and we went there on foot. After five days we got to the Barnstable lighthouse [at the mouth of Barnstable Harbor on the tip of Sandy Neck]. It was raining hard, and on the way we three went on board an old ship that had been wrecked by the lighthouse. When we were in the cabin, a little bit of a place, the fellow from New York was sitting on a stool, leaning back, when I shoved it out from under him with my foot, and he fell into some water on the floor. He was terribly mad, and was going to kill me, he said. We came to blows and at last I took a revolver from my pocket and shot him. The ball struck him right in the forehead and killed him instantly."

Goodwin said the third man, identified only as "Ainsworth," was "scared to death" and announced he intended to turn Goodwin over to the authorities. Goodwin, in turn, threatened to kill Ainsworth, "and at last he was afraid and we both took the body and buried it in the marsh.

"From that day to this not a person has known of it but we two, and we both started right back for Boston. We there parted and I came home. Every since I have had no peace."

Before making his startling confession, Goodwin had tried repeatedly to kill himself. "I have taken pulverized glass. It has killed other persons, but it did not hurt me. I have read of a man killing himself by sharpening a nail and opening a main artery. I tried to find [the artery] but could not. I then sent home for a book [on anatomy], and if I had been allowed to have it, I could have found it, opened an artery, and before morning be dead. I took verdigris [copper acetate, a poison]; that would [have] killed anybody else, but it did not hurt me. If I had succeeded in killing myself, I would [have] saved my wife and parents knowing the fact that I was a murderer. But everything failed, and now I can't help confessing the facts. I am a murderer. I am tormented day and night, especially nights when everything is still. I can't and won't stand it any longer. I killed him in cold blood and I am ready to hang for it. The sooner I am hanged the better it will be for all parties. Every word is, I swear, true, and I will take my oath on it."

Goodwin's confession was taken to the district attorney, who dispatched a state detective, Seaver, to Cape Cod to ascertain its veracity. Seaver found that Goodwin had worked on Cape Cod using the name Joseph Labouty.

There was no wreck at the mouth of Barnstable Harbor, but there may have been a ship that overwintered there. In the pouring rain described by Goodwin, he could have mistaken the craft for a wreck, particularly in light of the condition of many of the vessels around Cape Cod.

Detective Seaver returned to Worcester and interviewed Goodwin. When asked if his story was true, Goodwin snapped, "Well, if you can hang me before tomorrow night, it is; if not, it isn't." His churlish attitude soon disappeared, and he went back to his original story, swearing again that every detail was true.

Seaver did not believe him, but on the other hand, he could not prove the man was lying. While bodies frequently washed up on Cape Cod (something that didn't show up in tourist brochures), all those found around the time of the supposed murder had been identified.

As macabre as it sounds, Goodwin's only hope to be hung for murder would be if either the body could be found or if the mysterious "Ainsworth" would come forward and corroborate the story. That is how the newspapers got hold of the tale. The Worcester district attorney gave the story to the press with the hope that if there really was an Ainsworth, he would read about the case and present himself to authorities.

One thing the district attorney failed to mention was that Ainsworth had been an accessory to murder. Goodwin claimed that it only had been at the point of a revolver that Ainsworth helped heave the corpse into the salt marsh. Neither the district attorney nor Detective Seaver said anything about amnesty for Ainsworth, so it is probably not surprising that he never showed. A month later, Seaver announced that the story had to be false and as far as he was concerned the case was closed. Goodwin pleaded guilty to the break and enter charges, and was sentenced to the house of corrections, the death penalty not an approved punishment for busting into people's houses.

Almost a dozen years later, some hunters were scouting game a few miles from where the alleged murder had occurred. One of them discovered a skeletal limb protruding from the sand. The men excavated the bones. What they uncovered was indistinguishable from any other skeleton, save for the skull—the forehead had been punctured, as if someone had fired a bullet into it at close range.

Moving Violations

Moving Violations
Moving Violations

"You can't get there from here," is a
phrase popularly attributed to Mainers.
The same could be said for Cape Cod, where
transportation has always been, in a word,
terrible. For much of its history, the only
way to get around efficiently has been by
boat, and boats have a disturbing tendency
to wreck or sink. When roads were finally
built, they were poorly maintained,
frequently becoming a quagmire of sand.
When hard-surfaced highways finally
appeared, so too did the automobiles.
The Cape's traffic jams are famous even today.

The following tales are all about getting from
here to there, by boat or car or wagon or
train. We begin with those first tourists of
Cape Cod, the Pilgrims ...

The First Tourists

The First Tourists
The First Tourists

Imagine your community is visited by a busload of dirty, diseased foreigners armed with rifles. Their first stop is the local supermarket, where they grab whatever they can carry and decline to leave so much as a traveler's check. Next stop is your house, where they walk right in, open your cupboards and take whatever catches their fancy, all the while making rude remarks about your belongings and the food they leave behind. Then, on their way back to the bus, they stop at the local cemetery to dig up a few of the bodies, keeping anything they find of value.

A xenophobic nightmare? No, in 1620, that is exactly what happened. The *Mayflower* could very well be considered Cape Cod's first tour bus—a very low-class tour bus.

The *Mayflower* landed in Provincetown Harbor on November 21, 1620. The ship was supposed to land somewhere along the Hudson River to the south, but whether by accident or design, it ended up on Cape Cod.

The journey had been rough one for the colonists. The bad weather of winter had set in, so they decided to abandon their hope of making it to New York and instead established their colony in New England.

Four days after signing the Compact, sixteen men set out from the *Mayflower*, each armed with sword, musket, and armor, to tour Cape Cod. After wading through the gentle surf, the group proceeded single file along the shore. They soon encountered a group of five or six Indians with a dog. To their credit, the *Mayflower* company did not massacre them, probably because the first thing the Indians did upon seeing the colonists was turn and run.

The landing party from the *Mayflower* gave chase. They followed them through the dense underbrush that covers portions of Cape Cod, but soon gave up pursuit. The group decided to head inland to see what they could find. "We found a little path to certain heaps of sand, one whereof was covered with old mats, and had a wooden thing like a mortar whelmed on the top of it, and an earthen pot laid in a little hole at the end thereof," wrote "G. Mourt," believed to be a pseudonym for future Plymouth governors William Bradford and Edward Winslow, who published the story of the founding of Plymouth in England in 1623. The company dug around the sand mounds and came up with a rotted bow and arrows, which tipped them off that they were excavating around Indian graves, so they "made it up as it was, and left the rest untouched, because we thought it would be odious unto them to ransack their sepulchres."

Not so odious to the explorers was the stealing of the Indians' winter store of food. After passing through several small fields of corn, the company came upon a place where a house had been. They also found a ship's kettle from Europe, and "a heap of sand, made like the former ... which we digged up, and in it we found a little old basket full of fair Indian corn; and digged further, and found a fine great new basket

DEPARTURE OF THE PILGRIMS FROM DELFT HAVEN
From a famous old Dutch painting

full of very fair corn ... about three or four bushels, which was as much as two of us could lift from the ground ...

"We were in suspense what to do with (the corn) and the kettle, and at length after much consultation, we concluded to take the kettle, and as much of the corn as we could carry away with us; and when our shallop came, if we could find any of the people and come to parley with them, we would give them the kettle again, and satisfy them for their corn."

On the way back to their boat, the company lost its way. They came across a tree with a branch bent down with a primitive rope. It was a snare, one of the party figured. Bradford, who had been holding up the rear, came forward to examine the trapping device and ended up triggering it, and, like a bad episode of *Gilligan's Island*, it snared his leg. "It was a very pretty device, made with a rope of their own making ... which we brought away with us."

The party returned to the coast. A few days later, a party of thirty-four men returned to the cornfields, "digged and found the rest, of which we were very glad." They also found a little bottle of oil, two or three baskets of Indian wheat, and a bag of beans, all of which they took. "And sure it was God's good providence that we found this corn, for else we know not how we should have done."

While one part of the company returned to the shallop with the stolen food, another group set out to find the Indians, probably to pay them. They found not a soul, but came upon another grave, "bigger and longer than any we had yet seen." As odious as the task may have been, the group decided to dig it up:

> It was also covered with boards, so as we mused what it should be, and resolved to dig it up, where we found, first a mat, and under that a fair bow, and then another mat, and under that a board of about three quarters [of a yard] long, finely carved and painted, with three tines, or broaches, on the top like a crown; also between the mats we found bowls, trays, dishes and such like trinkets. At length we came to a fair new mat, and under that two bundles, the one bigger, the other less. We opened the greater, and found in it a great quantity of fine and perfect red powder, and in it the bones and skull of a man. The skull had fine yellow hair on it, and some of the flesh was unconsumed. ... We opened the less bundle likewise, and found of the same powder in it, and the bones and head of a little child. About the legs and other parts of it was bound strings and bracelets of fine white beads.

Somehow, these Pilgrims overcame their resistance to defiling graves. "We brought sundry of the prettiest things away with us." The group dug up a few more sand piles; all turned out to be graves.

While exploring, a couple of sailors from the *Mayflower* came across two Indian houses. "They having their pieces and hearing nobody, entered the houses, and took out some

THE "MAYFLOWER"

things, and durst not stay, but came again and told us."

Returning with reinforcements, the group explored the houses and found domestic items such as bowls, trays, dishes, and pots, and some not so domestic items such as eagle's claws, deer feet, antlers, and baskets made of crab shells. There were also several native delicacies such as acorns, fish, and a "piece of broiled herring."

"There was thrust into a hollow tree two or three pieces of venison; but we thought it fitter for the dogs than for us." And such small portions, too. A few days before, these colonists probably would have been happy to eat spoiled venison. There is nothing like robbing a few grain stores to cultivate a higher appreciation of food. "Some of the best things we took away with us, and left the houses standing still as they were."

Copyright, 1891, by A. S. Burbank

A VIEW OF PLYMOUTH IN 1622

After a couple weeks of pillaging Cape Cod, the time came for the colonists to decide where they would live. The Cape had been good to them, they decided. Provincetown Harbor was deep enough, there were plenty of good corn fields, fish, and whales. The place was defensible.

In spite of all the Cape had to offer, the *Mayflower* company decided to leave Cape Cod and go to a place they had heard about. Too bad they decided to rename the place Plymouth, as its original name was more appropriate—Thievish Harbor.

Barefoot Man with Cheek of Blue

In the wee morning hours of February 20, 1852, a stranger walked into Falmouth center, shivering uncontrollably from the cold. His clothes were soaking wet, and, though he carried a pair of boots, he wore nothing on his feet.

At the general store, he traded his boots for a pair of warm shoes. Of keen interest to everyone were his hands, which appeared black with frostbite. The man was directed to the town doctor, who fortunately did not have to amputate. The stranger lost his fingernails and some skin, but retained the use of his hands.

The newcomer gave his name as William R. Pitman. He said he was a sailor from Salem. Everyone he came into contact with asked what tragedy had brought him to Falmouth in such a wretched state. Later, when the locals compared stories, they discovered Pitman had not told the same tale twice.

Eventually someone figured that William Pitman must be related to Capt. Henry Pitman, a man who had been arrested

a few days before in Boston on charges he had plundered
the wreck of the barque *Missouri* of its gold and silver. Several
people in Falmouth noticed that William Pitman had carried
a carpetbag. While it could have held some of the stolen coin,
the total haul from the *Missouri* was said to be more than
$10,000. That could only mean one thing—the townspeople
would be going on a treasure hunt.

Dozens of men spread out along Falmouth's beaches
looking for some indication of buried treasure. It wasn't long
before they found it.

Col. Sylvester Bourne of East Falmouth noticed a shovel
and hoe that had washed up on the shore at Great Hill Beach.
He then canvassed the area and in short time found a stick
protruding from the sand with a handkerchief tied to it. As he
began to dig, a skiff filled with men who had just come from
Woods Hole pulled ashore to help. After a bit of digging, they
began pulling bag after bag of coin from the sand—fourteen
heavy bags in all, containing some $16,000.

During the treasure hunt, Pitman had left Falmouth and boarded a train for Boston. When he arrived in the city, two U.S. marshals arrested him. The carpetbag did, indeed, contain silver and gold coin. Once caught, he spilled the woeful story of his attempt to hide the treasure of the *Missouri*.

The loot had been stored aboard Capt. Henry Pitman's ship, the *Sterling*, docked in Woods Hole. William Pitman, Henry's brother, had been in charge of the ship when word of Henry's arrest came down in Boston.

That night, the stolen treasure was loaded aboard a skiff. William and his second mate, Clifford Dunham, rowed toward Falmouth, looking for a place to stash the loot. Upon finding the ideal beach, the men attempted to land the boat. However, the combined weight of the stolen coin and the two men prevented the skiff from making it over a sand bar. Pitman climbed out into water that came to his chest and transferred the treasure to the beach. Dunham returned to Woods Hole, leaving Pitman to hide the plunder.

Though his limbs were numb from the cold, he managed to dig a pit and bury the coins. He tossed the shovel and hoe into the surf and then began his two-mile walk into Falmouth. He had to take off his boots or risk having his feet freeze like his hands.

The case came to trial in April. Capt. Henry Pitman was found guilty, fined $25, and sentenced to three years in prison. His accomplice had been the captain of the *Missouri*, Samuel Dixey, who was likewise found guilty and, since he had wrecked his own ship to get the money, was fined $40 and sentenced to five years in prison.

And what of William Pitman? There was no law against receiving stolen property or, for that matter, attempting to hide said stolen property by burying it. It could be said that after his bout with frostbite, the authorities couldn't finger or nail him for the crime.

Dragging Main Street

Dragging Main Street
Dragging Main Street

O n Cape Cod in '77, there was only one place where teens and young adults could cruise: along Main Street, from Dennisport to West Harwich and back. Boys drove from as far away as Chatham and Hyannis every Sunday to see and be seen. In the ultimate display of horsepower, boys raced their rigs, screaming at the top of their lungs. Other drivers were content to just trot along in their vehicles, singing obscene songs and making rude comments to whatever female happened to be in the vicinity. Every Sunday, from afternoon to evening, this ritual of youth played out, in all kinds of weather.

For the residents and merchants on Main Street, the cruising became intolerable. In a letter to the newspaper, one resident complained "of rough and ungentlemanly young men, driving through our streets at a fast reckless rate, often wholly or partially intoxicated." The writer accused them of "using vulgar and disrespectful language" to both married and unmarried women who happened to be walking down the street. Furthermore, there are other men, he wrote, "who do not ride but congregate at different points on the roads, blocking sidewalks, insulting ladies with some vulgar remarks."

The writer concluded: "If the owners could witness the abuse their horses suffer, they would charge so high a price that none of that class could hire them. It is not unusual to see the same team pass the same point at least 10 times during the same afternoon and evening."

Horses? Oh, did we forget to mention this was 1877?

In spring of that year, the residents of Dennisport decided enough was enough. On the morning of Sunday, May 20, Richard Helfer and James Davidson were driving an open buggy down Main Street when Horatio S. Kelley, constable of the town and also the owner of one of the stores, stopped them. Constable Kelley ordered the men from their rig and placed them under arrest, then led them into his store and locked them up.

Kelly went home for an hour. On his way back to the store, he spied four young men gathered on the sidewalk talking about the recent arrest. The constable was still hot after his confrontation and arrest of the two men, and seeing four young men rubbernecking on Main Street did little to alleviate his condition. He demanded to know their business, and when told they had none, he ordered them to disperse.

One of the men, Arthur Chase, refused to move, citing his constitutional right to peaceably assemble. Constable Kelley's depth of knowledge of the U.S. Constitution may not have been up to Chase's standard, as he grabbed the man and took him to his store to join Helfer and Davidson.

Helfer and Davidson must have taken the same law courses that Chase had. Knowing that Kelley had no warrant for their arrest, they requested to exercise their right to post bail. "I've got you now and I mean to keep you," reportedly was Kelley's reply.

At some point, the constable managed to get in touch with a judge in the Barnstable court, who issued him a warrant against the men on the charge of "driving on the Sabbath." Under state law, carriage travel was prohibited "on the Lord's Day except from necessity or charity"—one of those laws that no one ever enforced. But it did give Constable Kelley the legal basis he needed for his arrest.

At 11:00 that night, Kelley loaded his three prisoners into an open wagon to take them to the Barnstable County Jail, twelve miles distant. Helfer and Chase, the two constitutional scholars, were placed in irons; none of the men were given a blanket or any other protection from what was developing into a chilly night.

The carriage reached the jail at 2 a.m., and the men were hustled into a cell. At 2 p.m., Chase was let go by Constable Kelley; Helfer and Davidson were brought before a judge. Their side of the story was that they had been on their way to church and, as the hour was early, decided to go the long way. They were stopped by Kelley, who, according to Davidson, treated them "in as insolent, imperious, and uncivil a manner as I ever experienced from any man who made any pretensions to decency."

Constable Kelley, in his statement, claimed that he was the victim of abuse and disparagement by the two men, not they of him. The judge found the two men guilty and fined them a dollar. They appealed the verdict to Barnstable Superior Court. All three men filed suits against Kelley for false imprisonment.

The arrest and fine had its desired effect on cruising the gut along Main Street in Dennisport and West Harwich. The ten to twenty teams that once paraded up and down the avenue slowed to a trickle. Racing stopped, as did men lounging on the sidewalks.

It took almost a full year for the cases to be resolved, but justice, this time, went to the cruisers. A Barnstable Superior Court judge in April 1878 dismissed the charges of driving on

Sunday. In a jury trial on the tort of false imprisonment, Mr. Helfer was awarded $82.08; Mr. Davidson, $63.41.

Arthur Chase, the "man on the street," won an incredible $480 against Constable Kelley, although the judge agreed to reduce the award to $300 and court costs if Kelley would pay it by June 1. Chase, a clerk in Dr. Ginn's Drug Store, now had enough money to purchase a horse and wagon for himself.

Cape Cod: Home of
the First Speed Trap

B ourne is the meanest town in the state," declared one
state representative (not from the Cape) at a hearing on
Beacon Hill in 1906. No one argued with him, not even
the Bourne town officials in attendance. All knew that Bourne
had the most effective speed traps in the entire commonwealth.

The automobile was just beginning its surge in popularity.
By 1906, 50,000 death-dealing horseless carriages were regis-
tered in the United States, most to persons of means. In the
summer, the rich liked to drive their cars to Cape Cod, and
they liked to drive them fast. Bourne and Sandwich bore the
brunt of it, for all motorists had to pass through those 2 towns
to get to the rest of the Cape.

The year before, the legislature had enacted speed limits
and given the cities and towns the power to enforce them. That
one act was akin to a declaration of war between Cape Cod and

Cape Cod Confidential

the "autoists," as they were called in those days.

In some ways, it was the Cape's own fault that automobile drivers were speeding through its towns. Beginning in the 1890s, Cape Cod communities began an aggressive campaign of road construction, transforming streets of dirt or loose stone into lanes of macadam (crushed stone cemented with a slurry of water and stone dust). Nothing slows down automobiles better than a lousy road, but the Cape was spending hundreds of thousands of dollars to smooth out the rough spots. At the same time, automobile-design technology was improving at a geometric rate. A decade earlier, the top speed of automobiles was around ten miles per hour. Within a couple of years, that had increased to thirty miles an hour; by the turn of the century, the automobile could cruise effortlessly at more than forty miles an hour.

As speeds increased, so did restrictions on that speed. In the summer of 1905, Dennis was the first to enact speed limits of 10 miles per hour. "When running through the thickly settled portions of the town or when approaching or rounding curves the speed not to exceed 8 miles per hour," the new regulation read.

With these new speed limits came fines, usually $10 per violation, and usually payable immediately. As most car owners were wealthy, towns were sure they would collect, especially since the alternative was impounding the automobile.

The gravy train would not last. Autoists accused the towns of enacting these restrictive speed limits for the purpose of fleecing unsuspecting drivers. The rich, in addition to owning automobiles, were also politically powerful. The aforementioned legislative hearing in 1906 concerned a law that would increase speed limits from fifteen to twenty miles per hour. The bill had come at the urging of the state's wealthy automobile enthusiasts. Elected officials from the town of Bourne showed up to be heard in opposition to the bill. At risk were hundreds if not thousands of dollars in revenue.

One of the speakers at the hearing testified that the problem of reckless driving fell to two groups: chauffeurs and intoxicated persons. Selectman George Briggs of Bourne disagreed. A short while ago, he said, a resident came to him complaining that "a lot of damned drunk automobilists" were driving like mad through the town, and he wanted them stopped. Selectman Briggs investigated and discovered that the party, which had been careening through the town, had been the Massachusetts highway commissioners rushing to catch a train.

Much of the hearing focused on Bourne's speed traps, which many believed were the most effective in the state. One of the nastiest was set up at the bottom of 2 hills, in the vicinity of where the Scenic Highway along the Cape Cod Canal is today. During a typical summer day, Bourne could expect as many as 150 automobiles through town, and more than a few would be traveling at speeds that frightened horses and pedestrians. Selectman Briggs told legislators that regardless of the opinions expressed, Bourne would keep its speed traps, "mean or otherwise."

His words proved to be a hollow boast. Within a few months, Bourne abandoned its speed traps, but not from the bad publicity of being named "the meanest town in the state." Instead, the traps had become a money loser for the town.

Cape Cod Confidential

To catch speeders, the constables from Bourne would set up their traps at different points each day along the town's roads. Each day, a group of local boys would find the speed traps and then head up the road a quarter to a half mile away. There, they would become the turn-of-the-century equivalent of the radar detector, flagging down motorists and, in exchange for a gratuity, informing drivers where the speed traps had been set that day. The scofflaw drivers would then slow down when approaching the traps and open their throttles once safely past.

Eventually the constables caught on to this tactic and began to turn their attention to catching the boys. They never could, and the first era of Cape Cod speed traps came to an end.

Murder in the Second

Not every murder on Cape Cod makes it to the front page of newspapers around the country. This book opened with murder cases that generated headlines as far away as Europe. The following rarely warranted so much as a headline outside of the Cape. Yet these are tales that capture life and death on Cape Cod.

Herein is another story about a body in a bog, but this time not a beautiful young girl; another child is slain, but not at the hands of religious fanaticism; another man is sentenced to die, but there is no reprieve at the hands of the governor. We begin with murder before the eyes of man's best friend ...

The Dog Lover Who Got away With Murder

The relative peace of a spring Saturday in 1892 broke with the snarling and snapping of two dogs engaged in a duel to the death.

One of the animals belonged to Richard Marston of Yarmouth, who rushed to the rescue and attempted to pull the two dogs apart. The strange dog, in recognition of Marston's efforts, bit the man so hard it drew blood. Marston responded in a manner consistent with a wounded animal. He lashed out by picking up a good-sized stone and hurling it, bonking the offending dog square on the head.

Later that day, Marston was passing the Yarmouth post office when a local tough, Charles Cash, challenged him. "What right have you to strike my dog?" Cash demanded. Another member of his family, Allen Cash Jr., backed him up.

"I have a perfect right," Mr. Marston answered, probably a little too firmly, as he was greatly outnumbered.

Charles Cash, who was much bigger, much younger, and a whole lot meaner, began to curse out Marston, using what witnesses later described as "all kinds of profane language." He then knocked the elder man down and began to beat him mercilessly.

Capt. Seth Hamblin was inside the general store when he looked out and saw Cash strike Marston. He raced out to help the older man, but was grabbed by the coat collar by Allen Cash, who recommended that he mind his business. Others came and were similarly warned to keep their distance while Charles Cash inflicted the worst beating that had ever been witnessed in Barnstable County.

Finally, Cash's bloodlust abated, and he and his entourage took off, leaving Richard Marston unconscious and bleeding in the street. Hamblin and another former sea captain, Isaac Gage, carried the beaten man to the doctor. "I have been to sea many years, but I never saw a man more 'bunged up' in my life than Mr. Marston was," Captain Gage said.

"The nose was badly fractured and the hip was lamed," Dr. Pulsifier said later. The left eye closed shut, and the face was mutilated so badly, some thought Cash had been using brass knuckles.

Cash was arrested and charged with assault with a dangerous weapon. The charge was later dropped to assault and battery when all the witnesses and even the prosecutor agreed that Cash had inflicted the vicious beating with just his fists.

The trial was postponed until Marston could recover. He never did. He didn't die either. He lingered for months, and then was even able to go back to work, although he remained in terrible pain.

Two weeks after the beating, Charles Cash was sentenced to one year in the Barnstable County House of Correction.

One year and a month later, Richard Marston died following an operation in Boston. He had been plagued by intense pain in his head and neck. A tumor developed on the back of his neck and he underwent the operation to have it removed. When doctors cut open the swelling, they discovered a mass of clotted blood beneath it.

The doctors could do nothing. Marston's health continued to deteriorate, and within a few days he was dead. Everyone was certain that the beating he had received more than a year before had eventually killed him.

If Charles Cash was guilty of assault, he was just as certainly guilty of murder. But only a few weeks before Marston's death, he walked out of the Barnstable jail a free man. He could not be tried for the beating twice, for that would have been double jeopardy.

Cash continued to live on Cape Cod after he got out of jail. It is not known how his neighbors treated him, but certainly they must have given him a wide berth. For one and all knew that Charles Cash was the type of person who would murder an old man for throwing a rock at his dog.

Who Killed Manuel Leo?

In the winter of 1896, they found his body in a bog not far from his little cottage in South Wellfleet, near the Eastham town line. Manuel Leo, a Portuguese immigrant, had been missing for six weeks.

Leo had moved to Cape Cod in the mid-1880s. He purchased half of a small house from another Portuguese immigrant, Frank Joseph. The two men lived under the same roof, but completely separate from each other. Neither had a social life, not even with each other.

They survived by performing the occasional odd job. In the winter, Leo worked for Washington Pierce, who ran an oyster harvesting and shucking business in Wellfleet. Pierce considered Leo an able man, a hard worker who could be depended upon.

Joseph died in the fall of 1898, leaving Leo alone. A few weeks later, in the middle of December, Leo disappeared. One of his neighbors came upon his house and found the front door left unlocked, something Leo never did. The key to the house had apparently been left in a basin in the kitchen.

Still, no one found this too terribly suspicious. A few townspeople made a halfhearted search for him, but turned up nothing. It wasn't until after the first of the year that some people began to worry that something had happened to Leo. In early January, several townspeople made a thorough search of the woods, creeks, and beaches near Leo's home. They found no trace of the man.

Two weeks later, some twenty-five Wellfleet men gathered to perform a line search. They stood twenty feet apart and walked from the beach inland in a straight line. They, too, found nothing.

On February 8, a Wellfleet man named Joseph Brown had been out searching for terrapins. He found Leo's body lying partly in a little creek not far from his house. The creek flowed into a bog hole some eight or ten feet across. Leo's body straddled the hole and creek, his upper body in the former, his legs lying in the latter.

Leo's body was stuck in the mud. When some townspeople managed to pull him up, they saw two things that shocked them. First, it appeared he had been hit in the face, where the nose meets the forehead. Second, when his hat fell off, it revealed a head of dry hair. If Leo had been floating in the creeks for several weeks, how had his hair stayed dry?

That was not all that was suspicious about his death. Leo's body was normal sized, not swollen like other corpses that have been submerged in water for any length of time. Also, there had been a large quantity of ice floating in the creeks in recent weeks. It would seem unlikely that his hat would have stayed on his head as his body moved between the floes of ice.

All of these clues seem to indicate that someone had put Leo's body in the bog hole only recently. Although no one would say publicly, the talk about town was that someone had murdered Leo and then hid his body. The murderer had pan-icked, however, as a result of the numerous searches conducted in recent weeks, and had placed the body in the bog hoping to convince authorities that Leo had wandered there in a stupor.

If it was murder, and that it was seemed very clear, the most puzzling question was not who, but why? Leo had no money, of that everyone was certain. He had lived a subsis-tence lifestyle for most of his life, although he had been seen a few days before his disappearance with a five-dollar bill. Still, that was hardly a sum to kill a man over, even a century ago.

Suspects were hard to come by. Leo had no friends, nor, for that matter, did he have any enemies. He was a hard work-er, although of late he had been subject to epileptic fits. Some people claimed that during these fits he would throw his clothes off, and once the convulsions left him, he would wan-der the countryside, his mind unbalanced. Surely that was how he died, some townspeople said.

An inquest was held a month later. The proceedings were conducted in secret. Some dozen witnesses were called. One, a Mrs. Boynton, fainted midway through her examination. The authorities never revealed what she had been asked that she had found so shocking.

In the end, no charges were proffered, no one was ever arrested. The murderer of Manuel Leo, a poor Portuguese immigrant, remained unsolved.

Therefore the question at the end was not, "Who killed Manuel Leo?" Nor was it, "Why would someone murder Manuel Leo?" The question, when the investigation was con-cluded, was, "Who cares?" If the end result is any indication, the answer was, "no one."

Deathly Afraid of
Breaking a Routine

As human beings, we find security in the routine and mundane. Change is difficult and usually a harbinger that something is wrong. For at least one young woman, change meant death.

A popular figure in Barnstable Village, Fannie Young ran the small lunch counter and newsstand across the Old King's Highway from the county courthouse. The lawyers, jail keeps, sheriff's deputies, and other county employees frequented her lunch stand, and when the court was in session, Fannie prepared the sandwiches and salads for the judges and clerks.

She fell in love with Merle Sears sometime before World War I, when she was in her twenties and he was eight years her junior. Sears's father was custodian of the jail, and Merle went to work for him as an assistant. The young man took his meals at Fannie's lunch counter, and the two began a long courtship.

Merle was not satisfied to follow in his father's footsteps. In 1919, he moved to Boston to join the Boston Police Department, which was looking for new men to replace those who had been fired during the famous strike. Merle found the regimented life of a police rookie not to his liking, and within months he returned to Barnstable County and took up a new career as an electrician.

He and Fannie also resumed where they left off. Their courtship, if it could be called that, stretched unchanged for more than a decade.

Fannie's life became one of maddening routine. As the years passed, she knew when she rose in the morning what her day would bring. She knew when she opened her lunch counter, she would see the same faces, for a local eating spot lived and died by its regulars. She knew that the late train would bring the Boston evening papers at the same time every night, and another set of regulars would come through her shop to get the latest news from the big city.

And there was Merle. Always Merle. Merle loved to play, but not to work, and more importantly, not to commit. By the late 1920s, Fannie woke up and realized that her best years were behind her. And despite her love for Merle, she knew she wanted to be married and told him so. "He replied he didn't intend ever to be married—said he wanted to remain free and independent as long as he lived," according to one account.

Having reached an impasse, the couple broke up. They remained friends, and Merle continued to frequent Fannie's lunch counter. They occasionally went for walks together, and newspapers hinted that their new relationship might not have remained completely platonic.

Fannie was pretty with an effervescent personality, and even though some may have thought that at forty-four she was past her prime, she soon discovered love with another man. Her new beau, unlike Merle, proposed, and the two set a date to wed.

Cape Cod Confidential

If Fannie's upcoming nuptials made an impact on Merle, no one could see it. If anything he became even more friendly and supportive of his former girlfriend.

Then, one cold winter Saturday in 1928, Fannie's regulars showed up at the lunchroom, only to find it closed. While unusual, the locked door was no cause for alarm. It was a weekend, after all, and Fannie had a wedding to plan. She probably had gone shopping in Hyannis or possibly even to Boston for the day.

That evening the papers arrived in their bundles, but no one appeared to lay them out. They were still there at midnight, when her neighbors called the state police.

There was only one trooper, John Dempsey, on duty. He quickly learned that Fannie had last been seen on the road to Hyannis. Trooper Dempsey, who had made many a visit to the courthouse and, undoubtedly, Fannie's lunch counter, knew of her former relationship with Merle Sears and that Sears lived in a house on the way to Hyannis.

Trooper Dempsey arrived at Merle's home in the early morning hours. Oddly, it looked as if every light in the house was on. He knocked on the door and got no answer, then moved to the back of the house. There he found a woman's body lying across the back step. It was Fannie, and she had been shot in the back.

Trooper Dempsey called for help. More police arrived, including State Police Detective Bradford. They searched the house and found Merle's body in an upstairs bedroom, a large hole in his chest. Next to him was a shotgun, which police surmised was both the murder and suicide weapon.

The authorities assumed that Merle had sent for Fannie on some pretext, and that sometime after she arrived they quarreled. When she tried to flee, he shot her twice, first in the arm and then in the back as she ran out the door. He then turned the gun upon himself.

Murder in the Second

Though Fannie's death was far from routine, it had come only when she tried to break the bonds of habit and regularity that confine all of us. And while she was ready for a change, those around her were not. And she paid for it with her life.

Dead Man Walking,
Cape Cod Style

Dead Man Walking,
Cape Cod Style

This is a Christmas story, although it contains none of the usual ingredients of goodwill toward men or peace on earth. Instead it is a tale of the evils of consumerism, an extreme example of what happens to some people who are bombarded with advertisements telling them to buy, buy, buy, when they have neither money nor opportunity to get it.

This is not a story of forgiveness, but one of revenge—an eye for an eye. It is a story that begins and ends with murder. It is the story of the only Cape Cod man ever executed in the electric chair.

It began two days before Christmas in 1931 when John Alves walked into his small cottage on Parker Road in West Barnstable and carefully hung up his sheepskin coat on a hook behind the kitchen door.

He had just returned from visiting one of his few friends, Joe Fernandes. The Fernandes' home had been an explosion of sound and motion, as if it were too small to contain

Fernandes, his wife, and eight children, not to mention the constant flow of family and visitors. By comparison, Alves's home must have seemed as empty as a tomb. Even though his house contained but two rooms, Alves alone could not even begin to fill them.

Alves had lived in his little house for a decade. Most of that time he shared the house with his best friend, William Pina, but Pina had passed away two years ago.

Nowadays, Alves had little to keep him company at home. He lived simply, but comfortably. On this day, he wore his normal uniform, consisting of a pair of old overalls. In the front pocket, next to his chest, he carried a small notebook, which contained a check for $45, payment for his work earlier that fall on a local cranberry bog.

Not long after his return home, Alves had to make a trip to the outhouse. He slipped out the back door, not even bothering to put on his coat. He had walked only a few paces from his house when he stopped, perhaps because he saw or heard something out by an old apple tree that grew a few feet away. "Who's there?" he called out in his native Portuguese. When he got no answer, he turned suddenly and rushed back to his house. He got only as far as his small porch before the blast of a shotgun knocked him down.

On Christmas morning, Conrado Fernandes rode his bicycle the three-quarters mile to the Alves house. Conrado was the father of Joe Fernandes. The elder man pounded on the front door, but got no response. He walked around the two-room house, peering in windows. From a kitchen window he could see Alves prostrate on the floor, his body surrounded by a pool of blood.

When police arrived, it did not take them long to piece together what had happened. Alves had been shot outside and his body dragged into the kitchen. The killer had rifled through his victim's clothing, taking the more than $100 in cash that Alves was known to carry, but leaving the $45 check.

Police recovered two spent shotgun shells from outside. Next to the body, they found a three-inch splinter of walnut that they were sure had come from the stock of the murder weapon.

Early on, suspicion focused on twenty-four-year-old Sylvester Fernandes of Mashpee, who was the brother of Joe and son of Conrado. Authorities learned that a friend of the Fernandes family, Manuel Rose, had lent a shotgun to Sylvester. When asked about the weapon, Fernandes claimed to have loaned it to another friend in Mashpee. When that friend denied the story, police returned to Fernandes and confronted him about his lie. Fernandes supposedly told his questioners that he had actually run over the gun with an automobile and destroyed the stock, which he had thrown away. Police searched Fernandes home and found the shotgun, minus its stock, hidden in an attic crawl space.

Police resumed questioning Fernandes, and in the late evening of December 30, he reportedly broke down and admitted to the killing. He dictated a five-page confession, which he then signed, police said.

According to the confession, Fernandes and his wife had been at his brother's house when Alves produced the $45 check. Fernandes had departed early, taking his wife home and then returning to West Barnstable to Alves's home, where he waited to ambush the man. After shooting Alves, Fernandes dragged the body inside, only to discover that Alves was still alive. That's when he clubbed the man with the shotgun, breaking the stock.

The next day he took his wife, mother-in-law, and an unidentified fourteen-year-old boy to New Bedford for a spending spree. He told his wife he had obtained a loan from the bank. There, he bought his wife and himself a coat and ice skates, and an air rifle for the boy.

Around Easter the following year, the grand jury indicted Fernandes for first-degree murder, a charge that in 1932 came with an automatic penalty of death by the electric chair. Some thirty-nine men had already been sent to their deaths since the turn of the century. If convicted, Fernandes stood an excellent chance of becoming number forty.

It took slightly more than an hour to select the jury who would try Fernandes, setting the pace for what would become a "speedy trial." At question was whether a "jury of his peers" would try Fernandes. Half of his jury consisted of two Thachers, two Bassetts, and two Ryders, three of the oldest names on Cape Cod. Quite the opposite was the Fernandes family, which had only lived on the Cape for seventeen years, having emigrated from the Cape Verdes Islands.

Fernandes's two court-appointed lawyers put up a spirited defense. Without the confession, the case against their client was purely circumstantial. The lawyers focused most of their efforts on keeping the confession from being entered as evidence. They tried to prove that Fernandes had been coerced. However, after the judge admitted the confession, there was little anyone could do to save Fernandes. At the end of his four-day trial, the Mashpee man was found guilty. The next day, a Saturday, he was sentenced to die in the electric chair at Charlestown State Prison.

Today, the average stay on death row is slightly more than ten years, mainly because of the extensive appeals. On the day their client was sentenced, Fernandes's lawyers announced that there would be no appeal.

Less than four months after his trial, Fernandes died in the electric chair. Throughout his trial and his confinement on death row, he maintained an inner peace that everyone who came in contact with him found remarkable. Father Ralph Farrell, the prison chaplain, had watched many men put to death; Fernandes was "the calmest man" he had ever seen.

Even more remarkable was that Fernandes appeared to have everything to live for. He had murdered Alves for his money so that he could buy his wife Christmas presents—his wife who had recently become pregnant. His child was born while he waited on death row. Fernandes had only seen his progeny a week before his execution.

During his final hour on earth, Fernandes wrote three letters, one to his wife and two to friends. Earlier, Father Farrell heard his confession and gave him Holy Communion. As he took his final steps on earth to the electric chair, he could be heard praying under his breath. "Jesus, Mary and Joseph, assist me in my last agony," he intoned. "Jesus, Mary and Joseph, may I breathe forth my soul in peace with you."

As he was strapped into the chair, he asked if he could shake hands with his captors. He then gazed at the witnesses, most of whom he did not know, and said, "Goodbye." A hood was placed over his head, and Fernandes could be heard resuming his prayers.

Eight months after the murder of John Alves, Sylvester Fernandes became the fortieth man in Massachusetts to die in the electric chair. Another twenty-five followed him, until the practice was abandoned in 1947.

"It is Me, Are You Not Frightened?"

Someone was terrorizing the Doe family in 1847. What began as a mysterious series of fires quickly escalated into the most horrible crime ever committed in one of Cape Cod's more gentle villages.

Jonathan Doe (not his real name) was a ship builder, and in the village of Orham (not the town's real name) he was a pillar of the community. He was industrious, hardworking, and fair to all. He employed people and was a leader in his church and in village affairs. He was the last man to have enemies, yet someone had twice tried to burn his house down with his entire family inside.

Three generations of Does resided in the home. Jonathan and his wife were joined by their son, Jonathan Jr., and his wife. The young couple had an infant son, ten weeks old, who was his grandfather's pride and joy.

The fires occurred in January and April. Someone had attempted to ignite the exterior of the house, but each time the fire was discovered before it did much damage. The arsons precipitated a wave of consternation that tore through the village, a sharp fear that somewhere lurking in the woods or swamps was a madman waiting for his chance to burn down the town.

On July 4, 1847, the Does discovered a cryptic message scrawled in white chalk on the front door: "It is me, are you not frightened?" No one got much sleep that night, anticipating that there would be another arson attempt. The night, fortunately, passed without incident, but for several days and nights there was always someone left to guard the house.

The following Sunday, Mrs. Doe decided to stay home from church, electing to spend the morning at home with her baby son. After everyone had left, and her baby had fallen asleep in a rocking chair, she went to make up a bed. When she returned a few minutes later, the child was gone.

In a panic, she alerted the neighbors, who in turn ran to the Baptist church to get her husband. The congregation, upon learning of the kidnapping, quit the church and the entire village soon turned out to search for the missing child.

At noon, Captain Rogers had just anchored his sloop in Orham Harbor and was coming ashore by skiff when he noticed a white mass floating nearby in the water. He set aside his oars, reached over the gunwale, and lifted out the body of baby Doe. Rogers's horror was so complete, he dropped the corpse into the water and could not bring himself to pick it up again. He rowed to shore and got two men to come with him to recover the body. Most of the village had congregated on the shore when the skiff rowed in. "When one of the men in the boat took the drowned child and held it up to view, a shock of extreme horror seemed to convulse every beholder," one witness wrote later. "And that promiscuous concourse simultaneously broke out in the most appalling shrieks of horror and dismay."

The terror that engulfed the village became magnified during the inquest a few hours later. The county coroner ruled that the child had died by "willful murder by drowning, by some unknown person." There had been no strangers in Orham that morning; therefore, the murderer had to be a member of the community.

The following day, the residents of Orham made their way to the Baptist church for the funeral. This would be no ordinary ceremony. Instead, each villager was led to the sanctuary, one by one, to the open coffin. There they were asked to lay their hands on the body and profess their innocence.

This was the trial known as "bier-right." According to some, God would point out the murderer, for when the guilty party touched the child, it would bleed as if it were alive.

They all came, and they all said they were innocent. God gave no sign. Finally, the only ones left were the Does. One after another, they placed their hands upon the dead child and denied any wrongdoing. The child's mother at first could not bring herself to touch her dead son, but when she finally summoned the strength to do so, she quickly blurted out, "I didn't do it, I didn't do it," and then snatched her hand away as if the body was as hot as the fires of hell. And that was when they all knew.

She confessed the next day to her mother. It was she who had tried to burn down the house, who had scrawled the message on the door, and finally, who had dropped her baby into the ocean. She originally planned to drown herself in a well, but for some reason she could not bring herself to do it.

Some attributed her dementia to a snake bite she had received on the heel when she was a child. She was mentally ill, a victim of monomania, of that everyone agreed. The family had her quietly committed to an asylum in Worcester. And for the first time in months, the village of Orham slept.

AFTERWORD
"LEAST SAID, SOONEST MENDED"

O f all the articles about Cape Cod crime and scandal that I have written over the years, I have found the final story of this book ("It Is Me—Are You Not Frightened?") the most unsettling. I first became aware of the "Doe" family and their tragedy when I discovered a series of articles about Cape Cod crime written in the 1930s by Donald Trayser. Trayser, a well-known local historian, had been a daily newspaper reporter covering the Cape. His series covered some of the same ground that appears in this book—Jolly Jane Toppan, Charles Freeman, Eddie Ray Snow—and sparked my future interest in the history of Cape Cod crime and scandal.

Trayser's version of "It Is Me" was called "The 'Bier-Right' Case." Unlike his other articles, Trayser changed the name of the family and disguised the location where the terrible deed was done. I found this odd, as the murder had occurred almost a century before the author put pen to paper. I theorized that

Trayser must have been close to the descendants of the family involved.

When I wrote my own version of the story in the summer of 1998, I made the deliberate decision not to change any of the names. The participants in this tragedy were long dead, and several generations had come and gone. I figured the family involved could handle a scandal that was more than 150 years old.

The article ran in several local newspapers on the Cape. A few days later I received the following e-mail:

> *Dear Mr. Albright:*
> *A recent article appeared carrying your by-line. I am writing to tell you that I am saddened to have this story revived.* [Johnathan Doe, the Orham ship builder] *was my great great grandfather.*

The psychic wounds of the murder of baby Doe had not healed over five generations, I thought as I read. The next few sentences stunned me:

> [Johnathan Doe's] *daughter-in-law was my mother's grandmother. My mother is 99 years of age and still completely lucid and alert. Dredging up the details of this sad story are not appreciated by me or my family. My mother, who remembers her grandmother clearly, had never heard the story. That my great grandmother was later released from the asylum and permitted to return home is a detail you have omitted ...*

I had omitted the detail because I was unaware of it. I did not know that the young Mrs. Doe had been committed, then released and returned to her husband. Furthermore, I did not know that she had more children and that she would live into the twentieth century to play with a granddaughter who would remember her with great fondness almost a century later.

Unlike every other story in this book, I have changed the names of the family and location in the Doe story. The horror of this particular tale is acute, and, apparently, still painful to the family involved. I hope the reader will forgive me this one compromise. The events of this story are true.

From this experience, I learned that Cape Codders are an extremely hardy and long-lived breed. They also have the shortest memories. My e-mail correspondent said that her mother's approach to life's tragedies was "least said, soonest mended." This very philosophy explains why so many of the crimes and scandals that appear in this book have been long forgotten by the local population.

Until now ...

ACKNOWLEDGMENTS

This book has been more than a decade in the making, and over the course of those years many have lent a helping hand.

Many thanks to Paul Kemprecos for contributing the foreword. Paul's a best-selling novelist, but he's never forgotten his Cape Cod newspaper roots.

I am grateful to the late Donald Trayser, who was the first to write about Cape Cod crime. Another inspiration was Michael Burgess, who exposed me to the richness of Cape Cod history and did important legwork on many of the stories that appear in this book. Noel Beyle and his amazing postcard collection have come to the rescue on many occasions. Several libraries were very helpful, especially the Falmouth Public Library, with its microfilm of the *Cape Cod Standard Times* and the *Falmouth Enterprise*, and its large, open collection of books on Cape Cod; the Sturgis Library in Barnstable, with its microfilm of Cape Cod's most esteemed weekly newspapers, the *Yarmouth Register* and the *Barnstable Patriot;* and the Boston Public Library, with its expansive microfilm collection of New England newspapers.

Thanks to former Barnstable Superior Court Clerk Phyllis Day and her staff, who were always helpful to a guy who wanted to poke around case files from the 1800s; and a special thank you to retired Dennis Police Chief Lou Cataldo, who will always be the king of Cape Cod crime history.

Cape Cod Confidential began as a newspaper column in 1996. It has been my pleasure to work with several editors across Cape Cod. A few deserve special mention: Karen Aude was the first to publish this rather unique view of Cape Cod history in the *Cape Cod Spectator*. After that publication folded, "Cape Cod Confidential" resumed in the *Cape Codder, Register, Mashpee Messenge, Sandwich Broadsider, Bourne Courier,* and *Upper Cape Codder* newspapers. My thanks to Edward Maroney and Ben Gagnon, and later Dan Hamilton and Seth Rolbein, all of whom took an editing pen to these columns in their original form (and in Ed's case, got to edit them all over again in manuscript form). Nancy Barry, formerly editor of *Cape Cod Life,* commissioned a longer version of "Jolly Jane Toppan," parts of which appear in this book. For the past few years, "Cape Cod Confidential" has been on the Internet (www.capecodconfidential.com). Walter Brooks, a true media madman, currently brings new "Cape Cod Confidential" articles to life on the World Wide Web. Walter's "Cape Cod Today" (www.capecodtoday.com) is hands down the best Web portal for news and information about Cape Cod. I will always be grateful that "Cape Cod Confidential" has found a home there.

Many thanks are necessary to Adam Gamble, who lived up to his name and bought this book for his company, On Cape Publications.

Finally, I wish to acknowledge my family—daughter Sarah, son Sam, and wife Lori—who suffered through this project for years, always lending their support and understanding.

BIBLIOGRAPHY

Everything in this book is true, at least as true as I can make it. The bulk of the information in this book was drawn from newspaper accounts. For certain stories, works published by others provided critical information.

Introduction: "The First Crime."—Samuel de Champlain. *The Voyages of Champlain*, Vol. 2 Boston: Prince Society, 1880.

"First to Fry."—Theresa M. Barbo. *Murder Hill: A True Story of Crime and Punishment on Cape Cod*. Marstons Mills, MA: Covered Bridge Press, 2000.

"The Cape Cod Vampire."—Leo Damore. *In His Garden*. New York: Berkley Books, 1981.

"The Cats Who Were Still Sniffing."—The account of Thoreau's stay in Provincetown is from his journal, June 21, 1857.

"The Berry Best Mother among the Pilgrims."—From the records of the Plymouth Colony, Court Orders.

"In Defense of Anthony Johnson."—J. Clay Smith Jr. *Emancipation: The Making of the Black Lawyer 1844-1944*. Philadelphia: University of Pennsylvania Press, 1993.

"The First Tourists."—*Mourt's Relation: A Journal of the Pilgrims at Plymouth*. Bedford, MA: Applewood Books, 1963. First printed in London, 1622, for John Bellamie.

Other Books from On Cape Publications

www.oncapepublications.com